Optimizing Supercompilers
for Supercomputers

RESEARCH MONOGRAPHS IN PARALLEL AND DISTRIBUTED COMPUTING

**Michael Wolfe**
Kuck & Associates

# Optimizing Supercompilers for Supercomputers

Pitman, London

The MIT Press, Cambridge, Massachusetts

Second Printing, 1990

PITMAN PUBLISHING
128 Long Acre, London WC2E 9AN

© M. Wolfe 1989

First published 1989

Available in the Western Hemisphere and Israel from
The MIT Press
Cambridge, Massachusetts (and London, England)

ISSN 0953-7767

**British Library Cataloguing in Publication Data**
Wolfe, Michael
    Optimizing supercompilers for supercomputers.
    —(Pitman research notes in parallel and
    distributed computing, ISSN 0953-7767).
    1. Computer systems. Optimizing compilers.
    Design
    I. Title
    005.4'53
    ISBN 0-273-08801-7

**Library of Congress Cataloging-in-Publication Data**
Wolfe, Michael Joseph, 1954–
    Optimizing supercompilers for supercomputers / Michael Wolfe.
        p.   cm.—(Research monographs in parallel and distributed
processing)
    Based on the author's thesis (Ph. D.)—University of illinois
at Urbana. 1982.
    Bibliography: p.
    Includes index.
    ISBN 0-262-73082-0 (pbk.)
    1. Supercomputers.   2. Compilers (Computer programs)   I. Title.
II. Series.
    QA76.5.W585   1989
    005.4'53—dc19

Reproduced and printed by photolithography
in Great Britain by Biddles Ltd, Guildford

# Foreword

This work was first completed as a Ph.D. dissertation at the University of Illinois at Urbana in 1982 [Wolf82]. In the past six years, the supercomputer industry has changed a great deal. In particular, with the recent replacement of the Cray X-MP computers by the X-MP-EA, none of the computers mentioned in the dissertation are now commercially available. I coined the term "supercompiler" to describe a compiler that would go beyond the current state of the art to optimize programs, since no compiler available in 1982 performed the optimizations described here. Now, there are several sophisticated vectorizing compilers that interchange loops and perform other high level optimizations. Some things have not changed, however; Fortran 8x is still just a proposal, though it has gone through a few more hoops and may be a little closer to acceptance (or not). The old joke that the "x" in Fortran 8x is a hexadecimal number no longer sounds like a joke.

In preparing this manuscript for republication, I have tried to update it. In particular, since this is no longer my dissertation, I have included the work of others, such as the data dependence hierarchy developed at IBM by Burke and Cytron, with appropriate credit. I have updated the data dependence chapter quite a bit, and have included some previously unpublished decision algorithms. I have upgraded concurrency analysis from a short section to a whole chapter, added a section about some special considerations for reductions, and split the explanation of the wavefront method into a separate chapter. I do not pretend that this is the final and definitive work in this area, but it has shown remarkable popularity, and I hope the update keeps it current.

I must express my gratitude to those who made both the original work and this update possible. My work builds on the work of others before me, notably Utpal Banerjee, who invented practical (or practically invented) data dependence testing. David Kuck supported me as a graduate student and an employee. Duncan Lawrie and Ahmed Sameh both aided me in many times of need. Mrs. Vivian Alsip and Mrs. Gayanne Carpenter helped me with many details for many years. Ronald Cytron, Ken Kennedy and Karl Ottenstein have served as friendly academic competition, and (I hope) have kept me sharp and honest. David Klappholz invited me to update and reprint the manuscript. David also read the whole book and found many errors. Any remaining errors are entirely my own. Finally, I thank my wife and family, who gave me the time to complete it. Thank you, Cindy, Jim, Greg, and Brian.

# Table of Contents

# Abstract

Supercomputers are usually meant to describe numerical computers that are designed to solve large scientific and engineering problems quickly. Effective use of a supercomputer requires users to have a good algorithm, to express this algorithm in an appropriate language, and requires compilers to generate efficient code. This book investigates several problems facing compilers for supercomputers.

One problem is building a comprehensive data dependence graph; we propose data dependence testing methods and we label the arcs with direction vectors that show the flow of data within the loop structure of the program. We use this labelled data dependence graph in several high level compiler loop transformations, namely vectorization, concurrentization, loop fusion, and loop interchanging. We show how to apply these optimizations for different supercomputer architectures.

We also investigate some problems associated with reductions and recurrence relations, including conditional recurrences and mixed control-data dependence cycles. A new formulation for the wavefront method of executing a loop is also given. Two other problems studied are the management of compiler temporary arrays and vectorizing WHILE loops.

# 1 Supercompilers

This book deals with compiler software for numerical supercomputers. Many scientists and engineers have tasks that require many millions and billions of floating point operations, such as weather forecasting, numerical wind tunnel simulation, even design of the next generation of supercomputers. To find answers quickly, these scientists and engineers use the fastest equipment they can find, often at the expense of ease of use. Supercomputers today are typically array-oriented, either using vector instructions or using multiple independent processors (or both). A recent development has been the introduction and commercial success of mini-supercomputers, which strive for high speed and low cost, to give a good overall cost/performance ratio; some manufacturers are now advertising micro-supercomputers and superworkstations, with lower overall performance, but also even lower cost. The explosion in the number of low-cost vector and multiprocessor computers can be attributed to the proliferation of inexpensive chips, such as fast floating point chips and 32-bit microprocessors, and the availability of a readily ported and acceptable operating system (the Unix system from AT&T). With the hardware and software problems reasonably well in hand, one remaining problem to efficient utilization of the resources is a good compiler.

At first, compiler support for supercomputers was dismally archaic. Now, research at the University of Illinois, Rice University and other places has produced a good theoretical foundation for automatic discovery of parallelism in programs. Where programmers were once forced to hand-optimize much of their code, using special syntax or machine language to utilize the special features of their machine, today's user is more likely to rely on the compiler for good performance. This is due partly to improved compilers, but also to the increased number of vector and parallel computers installed, meaning more users with less sophistication. Very expensive and time critical programs are still hand optimized, but many programs are sufficiently optimized automatically by compilers.

This book discusses several topics of interest in the area of high level compiler optimizations for vector and parallel supercomputers. This work is applicable to many architectures, including many currently available machines. Because the techniques are basically machine independent, we claim that applications programs, if specified at a high enough level, can also be machine independent; a suitably intelligent compiler can do a very efficient job of optimizing programs for the target machine.

This work has its roots in the Parafrase project at the University of Illinois; the Parafrase Analyzer was written to discover parallelism in serial programs [Leas76, Wolf78, KKLW80, KKPL81, KSCV84]. To perform parallelism discovery, the Analyzer builds a comprehensive data dependence graph which shows the flow of data in the program. This graph is used to carefully manipulate the program into a better form for the target architecture.

It was said that at some point in time, all programs would be written in vector or array syntax, and then the work of all automatic vectorizers would be finished. We believe this to be short-sighted; even with array or parallel syntax, the techniques developed for automatic detection of parallelism are useful in manipulating programs into a better form for the target machine [KPSW81]. This is especially true since we do not want to fall into the position of having all programs in a syntax designed for one architectural model, and having to translate them into new syntax for the next generation of computers.

The aim of this book is not to design an appropriate language for specifying algorithms; we believe that very high level syntax is easier for compilers to optimize, since it leaves more details to the compiler. The proposed array extensions to the Fortran language [ANSI87] are a step in this direction. Neither is the aim of this book to design a new machine to achieve the ultimate in execution speed, although we believe that the best designs will benefit from a methodical study of program characteristics and what code can be generated by compilers.

Improving the optimization phase of compilers for supercomputers is our goal. We believe that with the methods described here, optimizing supercompilers can be implemented that will fully utilize the potential of present and future supercomputers.

## 1.1 Current Supercomputers

This section describes some sample supercomputers and mini-supercomputers. It is not meant to be in any way complete, but is meant to show some of the architectural features that are important and of which the techniques described here can take advantage. One problem with describing specific computers is that the text becomes quickly dated; the descriptions shown below are of machines whose general architectural principles either have proven to be or seem likely to be widely used. We concentrate on those available commercially, as opposed to government laboratory or university projects.

**Cray.** The first commercially successful and widely accepted supercomputer is the Cray series. There are now many Cray models in the field (1A, 1S, 1M, X-MP, 2, Y-MP, X-MP-EA) and more on the way. All of the currently released machines have essentially the same general architecture. The main points are:
- High speed vector registers to hold vector data.
- Vector instructions to load, store and operate on data in the vector registers. Vector load and store instructions have a "stride" parameter, which is the distance in memory between two words to be loaded.
- Many pipelined functional units which can be simultaneously active.
- Memory divided into banks; vector loads and stores with a stride equal to the number of memory banks will execute at lower speed, since the memory bank busy time is several machine cycles long. This effect is especially noticeable on some models (Cray 2). Some models (Cray X-MP, Cray Y-MP) can have several memory instructions active at the same time.
- A "chaining" feature, whereby one vector instruction can use the result of a previous vector instruction before the first instruction has completed (not on the Cray 2). The Cray 1 had a fixed "chain slot time", at which time the second vector register had to be ready to issue;

the Cray X-MP introduced flexible chaining, where the second instruction could chain to the first at any time.
- Fast machine cycle time, ranging from 12.5 nanoseconds (Cray 1) down to 4.2 ns (Cray 2).
- Multiple processors sharing main memory, ranging from 2 (X-MP-2), 4 (X-MP-4 or Cray 2), 8 (Y-MP) up to a 16 in the future (Cray 3).

**ETA.** The ETA-10 is a successor to the Control Data Cyber 205 [CoDa81], which is itself a successor to the STAR-100. The ETA machines come in several models, with the fastest models being supercooled by immersion in liquid nitrogen. Air-cooled models are available with slower clock rates. The important features are:
- Vector instructions that operate on vector data in the main memory, which means that vector startup time needs to be paid only once for long vectors.
- Gather and scatter instructions to handle non-contiguous vector operands; operand vectors must be contiguous in memory for most vector instructions.
- Two vector pipelines, which produce 2 results per clock.
- Half-precision mode, in which each arithmetic pipeline can produce two results per clock, doubling the performance.
- A "linking" feature, in which certain triad operations, such as an add and a multiply, can be linked, when one of the operands is a scalar.
- Vector sum and product reduction instructions.
- A separate scalar unit which can continue to execute while the vector unit is processing vector instructions.
- Up to 8 processing units, which communicate through a Communication Buffer and a Shared Memory. The Shared Memory acts as a high speed disk for data transfer and virtual memory paging; each processor has its own private main memory.

**Sequent.** The Sequent family of computers is hardly in the supercomputer range, but it is a commercially available multiprocessor system. We include it because it is a good example of such a system. Its features include:
- Up to 30 processors (32-bit microprocessors).
- Shared main memory.
- Private hardware managed cache memory for each processor, with cache coherence hardware ("bus-watching" or "snoopy" caches).

**Alliant.** The last system we describe is the Alliant FX family of computers. This is one of the mini-supercomputers, and has several important features:
- Up to 8 computational elements.
- Vector registers and vector instructions in each computation element, much like the Cray computers.
- Shared main memory, like the Sequent computers.

- A single shared cache memory for all the computational elements.
- Hardware synchronization support.

The big difference between the Alliant and the previous designs is that the Alliant computers were really designed to attack a single job with multiple processors, where the Cray, ETA and Sequent multiprocessors are usually used for multiprogramming.

There are many other general designs to which the techniques described here may apply. For instance, the trace scheduling techniques used for Long Instruction Word computers uses data dependence testing [Elli85]. There are also a number of non-shared memory multiprocessors, such as hypercubes [Seit85] and systolic arrays [AAGK86]. Those systems may benefit from these techniques, but much additional work is also needed, so we don't pretend to be solving problems for those systems directly.

## 1.2 Parallel and Vector Languages

Historically, Fortran has been the programming language of choice for scientific programmers, both for its portability and because of the availability of optimizing Fortran compilers. This probably will not change in the near future, if only because of the investment in existing Fortran programs. The X3J3 committee of the American National Standards Institute has been working for over 10 years to update the Fortran language to make it more useful to the programmer; this revision is often described as "Fortran 8x" [ANSI87]. As part of this effort, array syntax is being added to the language.

The example programs in this book are in a notation similar to Fortran. We have taken some liberties with the syntax for clarity or to emphasize a point. We often label statements with names like $S_1$, $S_2$, ..., and label **do** loops with names like $L_1$, $L_2$, ... .

Vector syntax, a la Fortran 8x, is used liberally to show parallel or array operations - that is, statements which can be executed over a whole array or subarray in parallel. Colon or triplet notation:

```
A(1:N:2)  =  B(2:N+1:2)  *  C
```

is essentially equivalent to serial **do** loops:

```
do I = 1, N, 2
    A(I)  =  B(I+1)  *  C
enddo
```

although the translation is not always as trivial as those shown here (see Chapter 5). We will also use the **forall** syntax:

```
forall ( I = 1:N:2 )  A(I)  =  B(I+1)  *  C
```

which is syntactically similar to a **do**, but with vector semantics.

A multiprocessor computer can execute a concurrent **do** loop by assigning each iteration to a different processor. If the iterations are independent, then no synchronization is needed; if there is data passed from one iteration to another, then the processors need to be synchronized

4

at that point. If there are more loop iterations than processors, then each processor will execute several iterations. We use the **doall** and **doacross** statements to represent loops whose iterations are executed concurrently by multiple processors [LuBa80, Davi81, Cytr84, Cytr86]. These are described in Chapter 4.

## 1.3 Suggested Reading

This book was written as neither a tutorial nor a reference book. It describes many techniques that should be useful for compiler writers and others in a wide variety of applications. Those who are reading this for the first time, or those who only want to learn how compilers work (not how to write them) should not spend all their time studying the data dependence decision algorithms.

Chapter 2 describes data dependence and many other terms and notation that are used through the rest of the book; all readers should read through section 2.3 at least. Chapters 3, 4 and 5 describe vectorization, concurrentization and scalarization, which use data dependence relations to discover parallelism or tune a program for a computer; these can be read independently of each other. Chapter 6 describes loop interchanging, which is possibly the single most powerful optimization described here; sections 6.4 and beyond can be left for advanced reading. Chapter 7 describes reductions and linear recurrence relations, and can be read independently. Chapter 8 discusses the wavefront method, and depends on Chapter 6. Chapters 9 and 10 discuss some problems that arise when compiling for supercomputers; no rigorous arguments are given. Chapter 11 is a short description of some general design principles for supercompilers, drawn from personal experience.

# 2 Data Dependence

Two types of dependence occur in computer programs. Control dependence is a consequence of the flow of control in a program. Execution of a statement in one path under an **if** test is contingent on the **if** test taking that path. Thus, the statement under control of the **if** is *control dependent* upon the **if** test. Data dependence is a consequence of the flow of data in a program. The value of an expression is dependent upon the values of the variables used in the expression. Therefore, a statement which uses a variable in an expression is *data dependent* upon the statement which computes the value of the variable. Dependence relations between statements of a program can be viewed as precedence relations. If statement $S_w$ is control dependent or data dependent on statement $S_v$, then execution of statement $S_v$ must precede execution of statement $S_w$. In this chapter we will study data dependence in detail; other work [FeOW87] shows how data and control dependence may be treated uniformly by a compiler.

In ordinary computer programming languages, such as Fortran, Pascal and C, three kinds of data dependence may occur: flow-dependence (or true dependence), anti-dependence and output-dependence. We show how compilers can build a *dependence graph,* where nodes of the graph represent statements in the program and directed arcs represent dependence relations. We augment each data dependence arc in the graph with a *data dependence direction vector;* the direction vector encapsulates information about the **do** loop iterations at the head and the tail of the data dependence arc. A direction vector is a d-tuple, where d is the number of **do** loops that enclose both statements involved in the dependence relation. Each element gives the direction (forward, backward or equal) of the dependence relation in the corresponding loop. Computing a dependence graph with the associated direction vectors is a time consuming but important task for optimizing compilers. Compilers should not add arcs that are not necessary to the graph, since that constrains the transformations which can be performed, but it is even more critical not to miss arcs that do belong. Fast, strict, but conservative tests are required. This chapter describes a dependence framework and dependence tests that meet these requirements.

## 2.1 Terminology

This section gives definitions which will be used in this chapter, and gives examples of dependence relations and dependence graphs. Throughout this chapter and the rest of the book, we use $S_v$ to represent an executable statement in the program.

**Input and Output Sets.** For each executable statement in a program, there is a set of items (scalar variables or array elements) whose values are fetched (or potentially fetched), and a set of items whose values are changed by that statement. We use $\text{IN}(S_v)$ to denote the set of input items of statement $S_v$, and $\text{OUT}(S_v)$ to denote the set of output items of $S_v$. These sets may each or both be empty for some statements.

```
S₁ : A = B + D
S₂ : C = A * 3
S₃ : A = A + C
S₄ : E = A / 2
```

**Figure 2.1.** An example of straight line code.

*Example.* In the program in Figure 2.1, the IN and OUT sets are:

| | | | |
|---|---|---|---|
| OUT($S_1$) | = {A} | IN($S_1$) | = {B,D} |
| OUT($S_2$) | = {C} | IN($S_2$) | = {A} |
| OUT($S_3$) | = {A} | IN($S_3$) | = {A,C} |
| OUT($S_4$) | = {E} | IN($S_4$) | = {A} |

With array references in a loop, such as:

```
        do I = 1, 10
S₁ :      X(I) = A(I+1)*B
        enddo
```

the IN and OUT sets include only those array elements that are fetched or stored:

```
IN(S₁) = {A(2), A(3), A(4), ..., A(11), B, I}
OUT(S₁) = {X(1), X(2), ..., X(10)}
```

In practice, IN and OUT sets must often be conservatively estimated by a compiler, since the actual loop limits or **if** branches are frequently unknown at compile time. For instance, in the loop:

```
        do I = 1, N
S₁ :      if (A(I+1) > 0) X(I) = A(I+1)*B
        enddo
```

without more knowledge about N, the compiler must assume that all elements from X(1) to the end of the array might be stored (and A(2),... might be fetched). Also, even though the **if** may branch around the assignment half the time (or even all the time), the compiler must assume that the assignment might be executed for each iteration.

**Execution Ordering.** Classical flow analysis will tell a compiler what statements might be executed before what other statements. We use the relation $\Theta$ to denote the execution order of statements. We will write $S_v \Theta S_w$ if $S_v$ can be executed before $S_w$ (in the normal execution of the program). If $S_v$ is enclosed in $d$ nested **do** loops with indices $I_1$, $I_2$, ..., $I_d$, then we will write $S_v[i_1,i_2,...,i_d]$ to refer to the instance of $S_v$ during the particular iteration step when $I_1=i_1$, ..., $I_d=i_d$. If both $S_v$ and $S_w$ are enclosed in $d$ nested **do** loops with indices $I_1$, $I_2$, ..., $I_d$, we will write $S_v[i_1,...,i_d] \Theta S_w[j_1,...,j_d]$ if $S_v[i_1,...,i_d]$ can be executed before $S_w[j_1,...,j_d]$ in the normal execution of the program. While most loops run forward ($I_k$ is monotonically increasing), some loops run backward. In order to handle negative increments, we define the function $\theta(I_k)$ (where $I_k$ is a loop index variable) as any function that satisfies:

(1) $\theta(i_k) < \theta(j_k)$ only when iteration $i_k$ is executed before iteration $j_k$,

(2) $\theta(i_k) = \theta(j_k)$ only when $i_k = j_k$, and

(3) $\theta(i_k) > \theta(j_k)$ only when iteration $i_k$ is executed after iteration $j_k$.

A function that will satisfy these conditions is $\theta(I_k) = I_k$ when the loop increment is positive, and $\theta(I_k) = -I_k$ when the loop increment is negative. Notice that a loop increment of zero is disallowed.

---

```
      do I₁ = 1, 5
         do I₂ = 1, 4
S₁:         A(I₁,I₂) = B(I₁,I₂) + C(I₁,I₂)
S₂:         B(I₁,I₂+1) = A(I₁,I₂) + B(I₁,I₂)
         enddo
      enddo
```

**Figure 2.2.** Doubly-nested serial loop.

---

*Example.* The loop in Figure 2.2 has the following execution ordering relations:

$$S_1[1,2] \ominus S_2[1,2] \qquad S_2[2,3] \ominus S_1[3,2]$$

In fact, $S_1[i_1,i_2] \ominus S_2[j_1,j_2]$ whenever $i_1 < j_1$, or both $i_1 = j_1$ and $i_2 \leq j_2$. Also, $S_2[j_1,j_2] \ominus S_1[i_1,i_2]$ whenever $j_1 < i_1$, or both $j_1 = i_1$ and $j_2 < i_2$. We have used the function $\theta(I_k) = I_k$ in this example, since the default loop increment is one.

An important concept to bring up here is the idea of the *scope* of the program segment under consideration. If the scope is a basic block, then only those execution ordering and dependence relations that are valid within the basic block are considered; any loops around that basic block are ignored, even though they may add more relations. A compiler is usually concerned with optimizing a single invocation of a subroutine, even though that subroutine may be called many times within a loop. Also, loops are often optimized independently of other parts of the program. By setting the scope to a single loop, any other flow of control that may cause the loop to be executed multiple times is ignored. For instance, if the loop shown in Figure 2.2 were enclosed in yet another loop, then $S_1[1,1] \ominus S_1[1,1]$ for different iterations of the new outer loop. In all examples shown here, the scope will be clear.

The execution ordering relation is used to express the relative time in which the statements are executed. As we shall see, parallel languages have more tricky relations, since the time at which two statements are executed may be nondeterministic.

**Dependence Relations.** We look at dependence relations at the statement level. There are three kinds of data dependence between statements. The first kind occurs when a value

8

computed (stored) in statement $S_v$ is used (fetched) in some statement $S_w$; we say that $S_w$ is *data flow-dependent* on $S_v$, and write this as $S_v \delta S_w$. This type of data dependence relation shows how the data flows between the statements of the program. The second kind of data dependence occurs when an item is used in statement $S_v$ before that item is reassigned in some statement $S_w$; we say that $S_w$ is *data anti-dependent* on $S_v$, and write this as $S_v \bar{\delta} S_w$. The last kind of data dependence occurs when an item is assigned in statement $S_v$ before that item is reassigned in some statement $S_w$; we say that $S_w$ is *data output-dependent* on $S_v$, and write this as $S_v \delta^{\circ} S_w$. Finally, we say that $S_w$ is *control dependent* on $S_v$, if execution of $S_w$ depends on the result of some conditional test in $S_v$, and write this $S_v \delta^c S_w$.

*Example.* The program we saw earlier in Figure 2.1 has the dependence relations:

$$S_1 \delta S_2 \qquad S_1 \delta S_3 \qquad S_1 \delta^{\circ} S_3$$
$$S_2 \delta S_3 \qquad S_2 \bar{\delta} S_3 \qquad S_3 \delta S_4$$

It is often convenient to be able to ignore the kind of the dependence relation. We will often simply say that $S_w$ is *dependent* on $S_v$, written $S_v \delta^* S_w$. We also say that $S_w$ is *indirectly dependent* on $S_v$, written $S_v \Delta S_w$, if there are statements $S_{v_1}, ..., S_{v_n}, n{\geq}0$, such that

$$S_v \delta^* S_{v_1} \delta^* \cdots \delta^* S_{v_n} \delta^* S_w.$$

If $S_v \Delta S_v$, then $S_v$ is involved in a dependence cycle; we will see the importance of dependence cycles for vectorization in Chapter 3.

A dependence relation is a precedence relation. If $S_v \delta^* S_w$, then execution of some instance(s) of statement $S_v$ must precede execution of some other instance(s) of $S_w$. The data flow-dependence relations show the flow of data between the statements in a program. Data anti-dependence and data output-dependence relations are sometimes caused by coding practices used by programmers. Often, these dependence relations can be automatically removed [AlKe87]. Flow dependence and control dependence are sometimes called *true dependences,* since the other kinds of data dependence are false dependences that occur only when variables are reassigned in a program.

Computing the exact dependence relations can be very time-consuming or even impossible. We approximate the data dependence relations by using the following observations:

1) If $S_v \delta S_w$, then $S_v \Theta S_w$ and $\text{OUT}(S_v) \cap \text{IN}(S_w) \neq \emptyset$.
2) If $S_v \bar{\delta} S_w$, then $S_v \Theta S_w$ and $\text{IN}(S_v) \cap \text{OUT}(S_w) \neq \emptyset$.
3) If $S_v \delta^{\circ} S_w$, then $S_v \Theta S_w$ and $\text{OUT}(S_v) \cap \text{OUT}(S_w) \neq \emptyset$.

Note that the converse conditions are not true; in the program in Figure 2.1, even though $S_1 \Theta S_4$ and $\text{OUT}(S_1) \cap \text{IN}(S_4) \neq \emptyset$, there is no $S_1 \delta S_4$ relation, because $S_4$ can not use the value of A computed in $S_1$, but will always use the value of A from $S_3$.

Testing for execution order and set intersection is conservative (no dependence relations will be missed). Extra dependence relations may be computed by using this method, but most often (as in the example above), the extra relations cause no added constraints (by transitivity, $S_1 \Delta S_4$ anyway).

The real use of dependence graphs is to be able to ignore the ordering of the statements by paying attention to the dependence precedence. Nonetheless, it is sometimes useful to be able to distinguish between *lexically forward* dependences and *lexically backward* dependences. A dependence $S_v \delta^* S_w$ is lexically forward if $v < w$, and is lexically backward otherwise, assuming the statements are numbered from the top of the program down.

**Dependence Graph.** We often represent the dependence relations graphically. Not only is this a convenient way to view the dependence relations, but there are useful graph algorithms which can be applied to a dependence graph, such as finding dependence cycles (as we shall see in the next chapter). We represent the dependence relations for a program segment of a s statements by a *dependence graph* **G** with s nodes, one for each $S_x$ ($1 \leq x \leq s$). For each dependence relation between $S_v$ and $S_w$, there is a corresponding arc in **G** from the node representing $S_v$ to the node representing $S_w$.

The dependence graph for Figure 2.1 is:

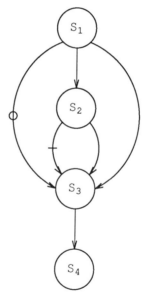

Here, we choose to have the nodes of the graph represent statements in the program. We could choose a different granularity for the dependence graph, by merging statements to get larger nodes, or get smaller nodes by going to an operator level graph. In any case, by convention, we do not add self-cycles to a dependence graph unless the head and the tail of the arc are for different execution instances of the node. If, for instance, we took the dependence graph above and merged $S_1$ and $S_2$ into one node $N_1$ and $S_3$ and $S_4$ into another node $N_2$, the resulting graph would be:

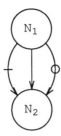

The dependence relation $S_1 \delta S_3$ is represented by an arc from $N_1$ to $N_2$; however the relation $S_1 \delta S_2$ is not represented in the dependence graph, since the tail and the head of that arc would be the same instance of the same node in the graph.

**Data Input-Dependence.** You may wonder what happens when $S_v \Theta S_w$ and $\text{IN}(S_v) \cap \text{IN}(S_w) \neq \emptyset$. In general, there is no ordering implied in this case, since it doesn't matter which statement, $S_v$ or $S_w$, reads from the variable first. A program transformation which reorders statements that are related in this manner can still preserve the results of the original program. However, there are cases when this relation becomes interesting (see Section 2.8); for this reason and for completeness we will say that $S_w$ is *data input-dependent* on $S_v$, and write this as $S_v \delta^I S_w$, when $S_v$ fetches some item before $S_w$ fetches the same item.

## 2.2 The Iteration Space

Informally, a loop can be said to describe an iteration space. A single **do** loop describes a one-dimensional iteration space, one axis of a Cartesian coordinate system. Each iteration of the **do** loop corresponds to a point along this axis. The **do** loop will visit the points along this axis in a specific order, as defined by the **do** statement. If there are two nested **do** loops, then they describe a two-dimensional iteration space, like points on a plane; $d$ nested **do** loops describe a $d$-dimensional iteration space. We shall use the iteration space for computation of data dependence relations in the following sections.

**Iteration Space.** We define the iteration space of a $d$-nested **do** loop to be a $d$-dimensional discrete Cartesian space. Each axis of the iteration space corresponds to a particular **do** loop. The space is composed of discrete points (as opposed to the real line, which is continuous) where each point represents the execution of all the statements in one iteration of the loop. We draw iteration space pictures to represent the iteration space, with the axes labeled by the corresponding loop index and with one point for each iteration of the loop.

    *Example.* The two-dimensional loop in Figure 2.2 traverses the two dimensional iteration space:

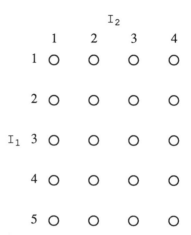

The semantics of the **do** loop explicitly specify the order in which the iterations will be executed. This can be represented in the iteration space picture by adding arrows to show the order in which the iterations are executed:

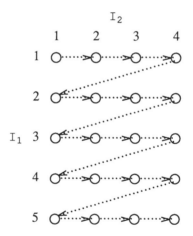

Certain transformation (such as loop interchanging, discussed in Chapter 6) modify the order of execution of the iterations.

**Iteration Space Dependence Graph.** We will also represent dependence relations in iteration space pictures. Suppose we have a general $d$-nested **do** loop with index variables $I_1$, $I_2$, ..., $I_d$. The iteration space dependence graph of the loop is an iteration space picture of the loop with a dependence arrow drawn from the point corresponding to iteration $\overline{i} = (i_1, i_2, \ldots, i_d)$ to the point corresponding to iteration $\overline{j} = (j_1, j_2, \ldots, j_d)$ whenever there exist statements $S_v$ and $S_w$ (not necessarily distinct) in the loop such that

$S_v[\bar{i}] \; \delta^* \; S_w[\bar{j}]$, for each pair of iterations $\bar{i}$ and $\bar{j}$ such that $\bar{i} \neq \bar{j}$ (as with dependence graphs, we don't draw an arrow from a point to itself).

*Example.* The iteration space dependence graph for Figure 2.2 is shown in Figure 2.3.

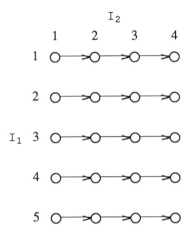

**Figure 2.3.** Iteration space dependence graph for Figure 2.2.

It is legal to change the order of execution of the iterations of a loop (change the order in which the iteration space is traversed) if the iteration at the tail of every dependence arrow is executed before the iteration at the head of that arrow.

Notice that iteration spaces need not be rectangular. In fact, one common type of loop is an inner loop whose limits depend on the outer loop index:

```
do I = 1, 4
    do J = I, 4
        X(I,J) = X(I,J) * 2
        Y(I,J) = (X(I,J) + Y(I,J)) / 2
        Z(I,J) = Y(I,J-1) - 3
    enddo
enddo
```

The iteration space has a triangular shape, giving this type of loop the name "triangular loop":

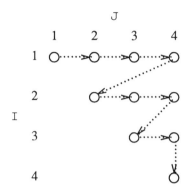

Not only are triangular loops relatively common in some numerical algorithms, but it is occasionally useful to create triangular loops from rectangular loops by *loop skewing,* as shown in Chapter 8.

## 2.3 Data Dependence Direction Vectors

In this section we augment data dependence relations with the concept of the direction of a data dependence relation and data dependence direction vectors. For brevity, all the definitions and examples are in terms of data flow-dependence ($\delta$).

An iteration space dependence graph resembles a picture of a "field" in $d$-space, similar to a magnetic field representation in physics; the role of the lines of force is taken by the dependence arrow. As in most cases, the dependence arrows in Figure 2.3 all point in the same direction. All these arrows could be described simply by describing the direction of the arrows.

If the dependence distances for each loop can be computed, these distances will describe the direction of the dependence arrows. For instance, in Figure 2.2, the distances are 0 in the **do** $I_1$ loop dimension, and +1 in the **do** $I_2$ loop dimension. In this loop (as in most cases), the distances are small constants. Sometimes the distances are functions one of the loop indices; other times the distances are unknown values, computed in the program. Thus, while the distance of the dependence is an exact way to describe the data dependence direction, it can be clumsy to find and represent in the general case.

A simpler but less exact description of the data dependence direction is the sign of the data dependence distance. The sign of the distance is positive if the dependence goes forward in that loop, negative if the dependence goes backward in that loop, and zero otherwise. The loop in Figure 2.2 has a data flow-dependence that goes forward in the $I_2$-loop.

We define the *data dependence direction vector* (or direction vector) to be $\Psi = (\psi_1, \psi_2, \ldots, \psi_d)$, an d-tuple of d elements where $\psi_k \in \{<, =, >, \leq, \geq, \neq, *\}$ and we say $S_v \, \delta_{(\psi_1, \ldots, \psi_d)} \, S_w$ (or $S_v \, \delta_\Psi \, S_w$) when

14

1) there exist particular instances of $S_v$ and $S_w$, say $S_v[i_1, \ldots, i_d]$ and $S_w[j_1, \ldots, j_d]$, such that $S_v[i_1, \ldots, i_d] \, \delta \, S_w[j_1, \ldots, j_d]$, and

2) $\theta(i_k) \, \psi_k \, \theta(j_k)$ for $1 \le k \le d$.

Each element of the data dependence direction vector corresponds to one of the loops that enclose the two statements in question. The direction in one dimension is independent of the directions in other dimensions. A forward direction ("<") means that the dependence crosses an iteration boundary forward (from iteration i to iteration i+1, for example). A backward direction (">") means that the dependence crosses an iteration boundary backward (from iteration i to i-1). An equal direction means that the dependence does not cross an iteration boundary. An asterisk ("*") is used when the direction is unknown or when all three of <, = or > apply. Data dependence direction vectors are a compact and convenient representation of the direction of the data dependence in the iteration space. As we shall see, they are sufficient to allow us to perform many very important and useful loop optimizations.

*Example.* We label the arcs in the dependence graph with the corresponding direction vector. The loop in Figure 2.2 has the dependence relations $S_1 \, \delta_{(=,=)} \, S_2$ and $S_2 \, \delta_{(=,<)} \, S_1$, and the dependence graph:

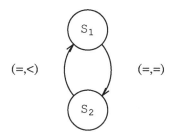

**Execution Order Direction Vector.** We can make the obvious extension to the execution order relation by adding a direction vector to $\Theta$. An *execution order direction vector* is $\Psi = (\psi_1, \psi_2, \ldots, \psi_d)$, and we say $S_v \, \Theta_{(\psi_1, \ldots, \psi_d)} \, S_w$ (or $S_v \, \Theta_\Psi \, S_w$) when

1) there exist particular instances of $S_v$ and $S_w$, such that
$$S_v[i_1, \ldots, i_d] \, \Theta \, S_w[j_1, \ldots, j_d], \text{ and}$$

2) $\theta(i_k) \, \psi_k \, \theta(j_k)$ for $1 \le k \le d$.

We observe that $S_v \, \delta_\Psi \, S_w$ can occur only if $S_v \, \Theta_\Psi \, S_w$.

**Legal direction vectors.** Not all direction vectors are possible. In Fortran **do** loops without jumps, the rules are simple. In a single loop:

```
        do I = L, U
S₁:         · · ·
S₂:         · · ·
        enddo
```

$S_1 \, \Theta_{(=)} \, S_2$, because for a single iteration of $I$ execution of $S_1$ precedes execution of $S_2$.

15

Across iterations, both $S_1 \Theta_{(<)} S_2$ and $S_2 \Theta_{(<)} S_1$, because execution of any statement in one iteration will precede execution of any statement in a later iteration; note that both $S_1 \Theta_{(<)} S_1$ and $S_2 \Theta_{(<)} S_2$.

Conditional statements in the loop can change the possible direction vectors. With the **if** statement in the loop:

```
        do I = L, U
            if (   · · ·   ) then
S1 :            · · ·
            else
S2 :            · · ·
            endif
        enddo
```

the relation $S_1 \Theta_{(=)} S_2$ cannot happen, since for any iteration of $I$ only one of $S_1$ and $S_2$ will be executed. On the other hand, a loop exit, such as:

```
        do I = L, U
S1 :        · · ·
            if (  · · ·  ) then
S2 :            · · ·
                goto label
            endif
        enddo
label :
```

will still allow $S_1 \Theta_{(\le)} S_2$, but now $S_2 \Theta_{(<)} S_1$ is no longer possible, since $S_2$ is only executed on a path that exits the loop altogether.

For an inner loop, the rules are the same as for a single loop when direction vector elements for the outer loops are all $(=)$ :

```
        do I = LI, UI
            do J = LJ, UJ
S1 :            · · ·
S2 :            · · ·
            enddo
        enddo
```

Here, $S_1 \Theta_{(=,\,\le)} S_2$ and $S_2 \Theta_{(=,\,<)} S_1$; as long as the direction for the $I$ loop is $(=)$, the $J$ loop can be treated as a single loop. When the direction for any outer loop is $(<)$, then any direction for an inner loop is allowed. Thus, both $S_1 \Theta_{(<,\,*)} S_2$ and $S_2 \Theta_{(<,\,*)} S_1$, since execution of any statement for one iteration of $I$ precedes execution of any statement for a later iteration of $I$ regardless of the relative values of $J$.

A compact representation of a direction vector requires 3 bits per element, with $d$ elements per direction vector. By using only three bits per direction vector element, we store the union of these direction vectors as: $S_1 \Theta_{(\leq, *)} S_2$ and $S_2 \Theta_{(\leq, *)} S_1$. However, some informa-tion has been lost by this combination. In particular, this combination makes $S_1 \Theta_{(=, >)} S_2$ as well as $S_2 \Theta_{(=, =)} S_1$ look possible. Two simple rules will alleviate this problem. First, only *plausible* direction vectors should be considered. In serial loops, as we have seen, the first non-equal direction must be a forward direction; thus, a direction vector $(=, >)$ is easily recognized as implausible. Second, we can store one more bit (the $(\neq)$ bit) with each direc-tion vector to signify whether the direction vector consisting entirely of equal directions may happen. Thus, we would store $S_1 \Theta_{(\leq, *)} S_2$ and $S_2 \Theta_{(\leq, *, \neq)} S_1$, signifying that $S_1 \Theta_{(=, =)} S_2$, but that $S_2 \Theta_{(=, =)} S_1$ is not plausible.

These simple rules are not perfect, but they catch the most frequently occurring problems and are practical, while still allowing the size and speed advantages of bit vector storage for direction vectors. The $(\neq)$ bit is also useful when **if** statements appear in nested loops. For instance, in the following loop

```
do I = LI, UI
     do J = LJ, UJ
          if (   · · ·   ) then
S₁:                · · ·
          else
S₂:                · · ·
          endif
     enddo
enddo
```

neither $S_1 \Theta_{(=, =)} S_2$ nor $S_2 \Theta_{(=, =)} S_1$; the lexical ordering of $S_1$ and $S_2$ is not enough to determine this.

Burke and Cytron [BuCy86] suggest a hierarchical representation of the direction vector, which is more precise but uses more storage and requires more time to access. We will use their direction vector hierarchy to compute data dependence relations.

**Vector and concurrent loop syntax.** In an extended language with vector and concurrent loops, the rules for plausible direction vectors must be modified. Vector execution of

```
forall (I=1,N) A(I)=B(I)+C(I)
```

means that all values of B(I) and C(I) are fetched, all additions are done, then all values of A(I) are stored. In particular, note that

```
forall (I=2,N-1) A(I) = A(I-1) + A(I+1)
```

and

```
do I = 2,N-1
     A(I) = A(I-1) + A(I+1)
enddo
```

will give different answers. The **forall** fetches all values for $A(I-1)$ before storing any value for $A(I)$; the serial **do** will store $A(2)$ when $I=2$, then fetch that newly computed value when $I=3$. When we use a block **forall**:

> **forall** $(I=2,N-1)$
>
> $S_1$:  $\cdot$  $\cdot$  $\cdot$
>
> $S_2$:  $\cdot$  $\cdot$  $\cdot$
>
> **endforall**

$S_1$ is executed for all values of $I$ before $S_2$; thus $S_1 \; \Theta_{(*)} \; S_2$, and $S_2 \; \Theta \; S_1$ does not occur for any direction.

Concurrent execution of

> **doall** $(I=2,N-1)$
>
> $S_1$:   $A(I) = A(I-1) + A(I+1)$
>
> **enddo**

means that each iteration of $I$ can be executed by a different processor with no synchronization. Since the different processors executing different iterations do not execute in lock-step fashion and there is no implicit synchronization, the results of this loop are non-deterministic. The processor executing iteration $I=4$, for instance, will fetch $A(3)$ and $A(5)$; depending on memory bandwidth, conflicts and external interruptions, these fetches may be done either before or after the stores for $I=3$ and $I=5$ (performed by different processors) have been completed. This means that $S_1 \; \Theta_{(<)} \; S_1$, as well as $S_1 \; \Theta_{(>)} \; S_1$; since the semantics of the **doall** neither require nor disallow these, we do not say that $S_1 \; \delta_{(<)} \; S_1$ or $S_1 \; \delta_{(>)} \; S_1$. Dependence is a relation that *requires* execution of one statement before another; the **doall** semantics allow but do not require this execution ordering, so even though a datum may pass from one iteration to another, we do not call this a dependence. Thus, in a concurrent loop (in the absence of explicit synchronization), the only direction possible is the equal direction.

The type of non-deterministic behavior allowed by our simplistic language definition may not be desirable in the applications world. An alternate definition of concurrent loops would disallow nondeterminism in the language, requiring the compiler to detect possible ambiguities. In this situation, the compiler would use data dependence tests to see when data might flow from one iteration to another (look for non-"=" directions) and flag these as potential hazards.

**Adjacent loops.** If $S_v \; \delta \; S_w$ and the statements are not nested in any loops, then we use a zero-element data dependence direction vector. In general, $S_v$ may be nested in $d_v \geq d$ loops, and $S_w$ may be nested in $d_w \geq d$ loops; however, there are only $d \geq 0$ elements in the direction vector, one for each loop that encloses *both* statements. For example, in the following loop:

```
        do I₁ = 1, 10
            do I₂ = 1, 4
                do J = 1, 10
S₁:                 A(I₁,I₂+1,J) = B(I₁,I₂,J) * D(I₁,I₂,J)
                enddo
                do K = 1, 10
S₂:                 B(I₁+1,I₂,K) = A(I₁,I₂,K+1) + C(I₁,I₂,J)
                enddo
            enddo
        enddo
```

the dependence relations are:

$$S_1 \; \delta_{(=,<)} \; S_2 \qquad\qquad S_2 \; \delta_{(<,=)} \; S_1$$

In some cases (as shown in Chapter 5 with *loop fusion*) a direction vector element is computed to relate the values of adjacent loops. As in adjacent statements in a **forall**, all iterations of the first loop are completed before any iterations of the second loop, so there can be a (*) direction from any statement in the first loop to any statement in the second loop for the adjacent loop indices. In this way, the J and K indices in this loop can be related by a direction vector element. The dependence relations augmented with this direction vector element are:

$$S_1 \; \delta_{(=,<,>)} \; S_2 \qquad S_2 \; \delta_{(<,=,=)} \; S_1$$

## 2.4 Data Dependence Framework

The framework we use to compute data dependence relations is based on the work of Burke and Cytron [BuCy86]. Given two array references (with s dimensions):

$$S_v: \; X(f_1(I_1,\ldots,I_d),f_2(\overline{I}),\ldots,f_s(\overline{I}))$$
$$S_w: \; X(g_1(I_1,\ldots,I_d),g_2(\overline{I}),\ldots,g_s(\overline{I}))$$

we test for both $S_v \; \delta^* \; S_w$ and $S_w \; \delta^* \; S_v$ simultaneously. The particular kind of dependence ($\delta$, $\overline{\delta}$ or $\delta^\circ$) that results will be determined by whether the variable references are stores (left hand side) or fetches (right hand side), and the direction of the dependence.

We will first test to see whether and under what conditions the array regions accessed by the two references intersect. Intersection will occur when the subscript functions are equal simultaneously:

$$f_1(i_1,\ldots,i_d) = g_1(j_1,\ldots,j_d)$$
$$f_2(i_1,\ldots,i_d) = g_2(j_1,\ldots,j_d)$$
$$\cdot \; \cdot \; \cdot$$
$$f_s(i_1,\ldots,i_d) = g_s(j_1,\ldots,j_d)$$

The conditions of intersection are a direction vector $(\psi_1,\ldots,\psi_d)$ relating the indices:

19

$$i_1 \ \psi_1 \ j_1$$
$$i_2 \ \psi_2 \ j_2$$
$$.\quad.\quad.$$
$$i_d \ \psi_d \ j_d$$

We first test for intersection with a direction vector $(*, *, \ldots, *)$. If independence can be proven with this direction vector, then the regions accessed by the two references are disjoint. If independence is not proven, then one "$*$" direction vector element is refined to "$<$", "$=$" and "$>$". Thus, intersection testing is done on a hierarchy of direction vectors. If independence can be proven at any point in the hierarchy, the direction vectors beneath it need not be tested. The hierarchy for two loops is:

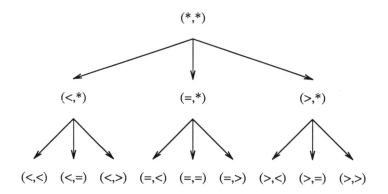

We define the complement of a direction vector $\Psi = (\psi_1, \ldots, \psi_d)$ to be $\Psi^{-1} = (\psi_1^{-1}, \ldots, \psi_d^{-1})$, where each $\psi_k^{-1}$ is computed from $\psi_k$ as follows:

| $\psi_k$ | $<$ | $=$ | $>$ | $\leq$ | $\geq$ | $\neq$ | $*$ |
|---|---|---|---|---|---|---|---|
| $\psi_k^{-1}$ | $>$ | $=$ | $<$ | $\geq$ | $\leq$ | $\neq$ | $*$ |

$\Psi^{-1}$ is the same as $\Psi$ with the $<$ and $>$ reversed. We also define the intersection of two direction vectors as follows: Given two direction vectors $\Psi^1 = (\psi_1^1, \ldots, \psi_d^1)$ and $\Psi^2 = (\psi_1^2, \ldots, \psi_d^2)$, we find

$$\Psi = (\psi_1, \ldots, \psi_d) = \Psi^1 \times \Psi^2$$

by computing:

$$\psi_1 = \psi_1^1 \times \psi_1^2, \quad \psi_2 = \psi_2^1 \times \psi_2^2, \quad \ldots, \quad \psi_d = \psi_d^1 \times \psi_d^2$$

where the $\times$ operation on direction vector elements is defined as follows:

| $\times$ | < | = | > | ≤ | ≥ | ≠ | * |
|---|---|---|---|---|---|---|---|
| < | < | . | . | < | . | < | < |
| = | . | = | . | = | = | . | = |
| > | . | . | > | . | > | > | > |
| ≤ | < | = | . | ≤ | = | < | ≤ |
| ≥ | . | = | > | = | ≥ | > | ≥ |
| ≠ | < | . | > | < | > | ≠ | ≠ |
| * | < | = | > | ≤ | ≥ | ≠ | * |

If the direction vectors are stored as bit vectors, with three bits for each direction vector element (one bit each for <, = and >), intersection is quickly computed by ANDing the bit vectors. The "." entries in the table mean that the result is a null direction vector element.

When we perform intersection testing, we test each subscript individually; this produces one direction vector $\Psi_k$ for each subscript. Since intersection requires simultaneous intersection in all subscripts, we can combine the different direction vectors to get one direction vector $\Psi$:

$$\Psi = \Psi_1 \times \Psi_2 \times \cdot \cdot \cdot \times \Psi_s$$

If this combination produces any "." entries, then there is no simultaneous intersection at all and so there can be no dependence.

To convert this subscript intersection into a data dependence, we must also take into account the execution ordering. So we must find the direction vectors $\Omega_{v \to w}$ and $\Omega_{w \to v}$ that satisfy:

$$S_v \ \Theta_{\Omega_{v \to w}} \ S_w \quad \text{and} \ S_w \ \Theta_{\Omega_{w \to v}} \ S_v$$

To get the data dependence direction vector for dependence from $S_v$ to $S_w$, we intersect $\Psi$ with $\Omega_{v \to w}$ to get $\Psi_{v \to w}$:

$$\Psi_{v \to w} = \Psi \times \Omega_{v \to w}$$

Again, if this combination produces any "." entries, there is no dependence from $S_v$ to $S_w$. If all entries are valid, we add the data dependence relation:

$$S_v \ \delta^*_{\Psi_{v \to w}} \ S_w$$

to our dependence graph. The actual kind of dependence ($\delta$, $\bar{\delta}$ or $\delta^\circ$) will be determined by the type of reference in question. If the reference in $S_v$ is in OUT($S_v$), while the reference in $S_w$ is in IN($S_w$), then this relation is a data flow-dependence ($\delta$); the converse implies a data anti-dependence ($\bar{\delta}$). If both references are in the OUT sets, then the relation is a data output-dependence ($\delta^\circ$).

Similarly, to compute dependence from $S_w$ to $S_v$ we intersect $\Psi^{-1}$ with $\Omega_{w \to v}$; we must use $\Psi^{-1}$ here since $\Psi$ is computed for intersection from $S_v$ to $S_w$.

$$\Psi_{w \to v} = \Psi^{-1} \times \Omega_{w \to v}$$

If all entries are valid we add the dependence relation

$$S_w \ \overset{*}{\delta}_{\Psi_{w \to v}} \ S_v$$

## 2.5 Data Dependence Decision Algorithms

The decision algorithms used here will find whether two linear subscript functions can intersect under the constraints of a direction vector and the loop limits. These methods are modifications of Banerjee's algorithms ([Bane76, Bane79]), and have been adapted to find data dependence direction vectors. In this section we use the following notation throughout:

Let $S_v$ and $S_w$ be nested in $d$ loops with indices $\overline{I} = (I_1,...,I_d)$ that have loop limits:

$$\textbf{do} \ I_k = L_k, \ U_k, \ N_k$$

Let $f$ and $g$ be functions of $\overline{I}$ used as some subscript function of some array $X$ in $S_v$ and $S_w$, and suppose

$$f(\overline{I}) = A_0 + \sum_{k=1}^{d} A_k I_k \quad \text{and} \quad g(\overline{I}) = B_0 + \sum_{k=1}^{d} B_k I_k.$$

Let $\Psi = (\psi_1, \ldots, \psi_d)$ be a direction vector, and let $\Gamma(\Psi, \omega) = \{k \mid \psi_k \equiv \omega\}$ where $\omega \in \{<, =, >, \le, \ge, \ne, *\}$.

So we have a program segment like:

$$\textbf{do} \ I_1 = L_1, \ U_1, \ N_1$$
$$\cdots$$
$$\textbf{do} \ I_d = L_d, \ U_d, \ N_d$$

$S_v$ :          $\cdots \ X(\ldots, f(I_1, \ldots, I_d), \ldots) \ \cdots$

$S_w$ :          $\cdots \ X(\ldots, g(I_1, \ldots, I_d), \ldots) \ \cdots$

$$\textbf{enddo}$$
$$\cdots$$
$$\textbf{enddo}$$

We try to find solutions $\overline{i}$ and $\overline{j}$ for $\overline{I}$ that satisfy the dependence equation:

$$f(\overline{i}) = g(\overline{j})$$

such that the direction vector is also satisfied:

$$\theta(i_k) \ \psi_k \ \theta(j_k)$$

We sometimes used a normalized index $I_k^n$ instead of $I_k$, where:

$$I_k = I_k^n N_k + L_k .$$

The normalized index $I_k^n$ satisfies the inequality

$$0 \leq I_k^n \leq (U_k - L_k) / N_k$$

and has an increment of one. Note that a valid choice for $\theta(I_k)$ is $I_k^n$ regardless of the sign of the increment $N_k$. We can also express $f$ and $g$ in terms of the normalized index set:

$$f^n(\overline{I}^n) = A_0 + \sum_{k=1}^{d} A_k N_k I_k^n + \sum_{k=1}^{d} A_k L_k$$
$$g^n(\overline{I}^n) = B_0 + \sum_{k=1}^{d} B_k N_k I_k^n + \sum_{k=1}^{d} B_k L_k .$$

An equivalent problem is to find solutions $\overline{i}^n$ and $\overline{j}^n$ for $\overline{I}^n$ that satisfy the normalized dependence equation:

$$f^n(\overline{i}^n) = g^n(\overline{j}^n)$$

such that the direction vector is satisfied (choosing $\theta(I_k) = I_k^n$):

$$i_k^n \ \psi_k \ j_k^n$$

## 2.5.1 GCD Test

The GCD test is a simple test which can detect independence, and is included for completeness [Towl76, Bane76, AlKe87]. The test can be stated as:

*The normalized dependence equation is satisfied only when*
$$\text{GCD}(\{ (A_k - B_k) N_k : k \in \Gamma(\Psi, =) \}, \{ A_k N_k , B_k N_k : k \notin \Gamma(\Psi, =) \})$$
*divides* $B_0 - A_0 + \sum_{k=1}^{d} (B_k - A_k) L_k$

**Proof.** The normalized dependence equation is equivalent to

$$\sum_{k=1}^{d} (A_k N_k i_k^n - B_k N_k j_k^n) = B_0 - A_0 + \sum_{k=1}^{d} (B_k - A_k) L_k$$

or

$$\sum_{k \in \Gamma(\Psi, =)} (A_k - B_k) N_k i_k^n + \sum_{k \notin \Gamma(\Psi, =)} (A_k N_k i_k^n - B_k N_k j_k^n) = B_0 - A_0 + \sum_{k=1}^{d} (B_k - A_k) L_k$$

By the theory of Diophantine equations [Grif54] this has an integer solution only if the GCD test succeeds.

In the most common cases where $A_k = B_k$ for all $k$, this reduces to

$$\text{GCD}(\{ A_k N_k : k \notin \Gamma(\Psi, =) \}) \ | \ B_0 - A_0$$

**Weak GCD Test.** Notice that the loop lower limit $L_k$ is needed for the GCD test; this is unfortunate since loop lower limits are frequently variables. Luckily, the $(B_k - A_k) L_k$ term drops out whenever $B_k = A_k$, and so $L_k$ is not needed for those loops. Notice also that the loop increment is needed; if the loop increment is a variable or unknown expression, a weaker GCD test can be used:

*The dependence equation is satisfied only when*

$$\text{GCD}(\{(A_k - B_k) : k \in \Gamma(\Psi, =)\}, \{A_k, B_k : k \notin \Gamma(\Psi, =)\}) \mid B_0 - A_0$$

**Proof.** Same as above.

The GCD test is quick, but is in practice relatively ineffective. In most subscripts the loop index multipliers $A_k = B_k = 1$ and the increment $N_k = 1$, so the GCD is one. It is useful in cases such as:

```
       do I = 1, 10, 2
S₁:       X(I) = ...
S₂:       ... = X(I+1)
       enddo
```

Here, the GCD is 2, which does not divide the difference, which is 1; since there are no integer solutions, there can be no dependence.

## 2.5.2 Banerjee's Inequality

One of the more popular data dependence decision algorithms is commonly called Banerjee's Inequality [Bane76, BCKT79]. It has been studied extensively in the literature and modified for several different purposes [Alle83, AlKe84, AlKe87, Elli85]. Here, we modify Banerjee's original work in order to discover whether a dependence relation exists with a particular direction vector.

First, we must define some new notation. We define the *positive part* of a real number $r$, $r^+$, and the *negative part* of $r$, $r^-$, as:

$$r^+ = \begin{cases} 0, & r < 0 \\ r, & r \geq 0 \end{cases}$$

$$r^- = \begin{cases} r, & r \leq 0 \\ 0, & r > 0 \end{cases}$$

If $r$, $s$ and $z$ are real numbers with $0 \leq z \leq s$, then the following properties hold:
a)  $r^+ \geq 0$, $r^- \leq 0$
b)  $r = r^+ + r^-$
c)  $(-r)^+ = -r^-$, $(-r)^- = -r^+$
d)  $r^- s \leq rz \leq r^+ s$
e)  $-r^- s \geq -rz \geq -r^+ s$

(In Banerjee's original work and other work on Banerjee's inequalities, $r^-$ was $|r|$ or 0; here we invert the sign of $r^-$ to make the bounds equations somewhat simpler).

Now we present the essence of Banerjee's Inequalities. Given functions $f$ and $g$ and a direction vector $\Psi$ as above, we try to find whether $f(\bar{i}) = g(\bar{j})$ can be found for some $\bar{i}, \bar{j}$ under the constraints of the direction vector $\Psi$ and the loop limits. The dependence equation is:

$$\sum_{k=1}^{d} (A_k i_k - B_k j_k) = B_0 - A_0,$$

For each value of $k$, find a lower and upper bound such that:

$$LB_k^{\Psi_k} \leq A_k i_k - B_k j_k \leq UB_k^{\Psi_k}$$

The lower and upper bounds depend not only on the loop limits, but on the particular direction vector element. By summing these bounds, we have the inequality:

$$\sum_{k=1}^{d} LB_k^{\Psi_k} \leq \sum_{k=1}^{d} (A_k i_k - B_k j_k) \leq \sum_{k=1}^{d} UB_k^{\Psi_k}$$

or, equivalently

$$\sum_{k=1}^{d} LB_k^{\Psi_k} \leq B_0 - A_0 \leq \sum_{k=1}^{d} UB_k^{\Psi_k}$$

If either $\sum_{k=1}^{d} LB_k^{\Psi_k} > B_0 - A_0$ or $\sum_{k=1}^{d} UB_k^{\Psi_k} < B_0 - A_0$ is true, then the functions can not intersect under the constraints of the direction vector. In the explanation below we assume that $N_k > 0$; if $N_k < 0$, then use $\psi^{-1}$ to choose the proper case below, switching $L_k$ and $U_k$ and using the absolute value of $N_k$.

$\Psi_k \equiv <$

$$LB_k^< = (A_k^- - B_k)^- (U_k - L_k - N_k) + (A_k - B_k) L_k - B_k N_k$$
$$UB_k^< = (A_k^+ - B_k)^+ (U_k - L_k - N_k) + (A_k - B_k) L_k - B_k N_k$$

$\Psi_k \equiv =$

$$LB_k^= = (A_k - B_k)^- (U_k - L_k) + (A_k - B_k) L_k$$
$$UB_k^= = (A_k - B_k)^+ (U_k - L_k) + (A_k - B_k) L_k$$

$\Psi_k \equiv >$

$$LB_k^> = (A_k - B_k^+)^- (U_k - L_k - N_k) + (A_k - B_k) L_k + A_k N_k$$
$$UB_k^> = (A_k - B_k^-)^+ (U_k - L_k - N_k) + (A_k - B_k) L_k + A_k N_k$$

$\Psi_k \equiv *$

$$LB_k^* = (A_k^- - B_k^+) (U_k - L_k) + (A_k - B_k) L_k$$
$$UB_k^* = (A_k^+ - B_k^-) (U_k - L_k) + (A_k - B_k) L_k$$

We show how one of these bounds is derived below; the rest of the derivations are essentially similar:

$\psi_k \equiv <$

$$i_k < j_k$$

$$0 \le i_k - L_k < j_k - L_k \le U_k - L_k \$$$

$$0 \le i_k - L_k \le j_k - L_k - N_k \le U_k - L_k - N_k \$$$

$$A_k i_k - B_k j_k = A_k (i_k - L_k) - B_k (j_k - L_k - N_k) + (A_k L_k - B_k L_k - B_k N_k)$$

$$\le A_k^+ (j_k - L_k - N_k) - B_k (j_k - L_k - N_k) + (A_k - B_k) L_k - B_k N_k \qquad \text{(rule d)}$$

$$\le (A_k^+ - B_k) (j_k - L_k - N_k) + (A_k - B_k) L_k - B_k N_k$$

$$\le (A_k^+ - B_k)^+ (U_k - L_k - N_k)^+ + (A_k - B_k) L_k - B_k N_k = UB_k^< \qquad \text{(rule d)}$$

*Example.* We will show how these bounds work by computing the dependence relations for the following loop:

```
do I = 1, 10
    do J = 1, 10
S₁:        A(I*10+J)  = ...
S₂:        ...  = A(I*10+J-1)
    enddo
enddo
```

For simplicity, we will precompute all the possible lower and upper bounds:

$$LB_I^* = -90 \quad LB_I^< = -90 \quad LB_I^= = 0 \quad LB_I^> = 10$$
$$UB_I^* = 90 \quad UB_I^< = -10 \quad UB_I^= = 0 \quad UB_I^> = 90$$
$$LB_J^* = -9 \quad LB_J^< = -9 \quad LB_J^= = 0 \quad LB_J^> = 1$$
$$UB_J^* = 9 \quad UB_J^< = -1 \quad UB_J^= = 0 \quad UB_J^> = 9$$

We now compute the dependence hierarchy below:

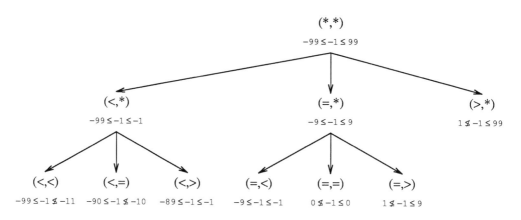

Note that for the direction $(>, *)$ the relation $1 \le -1$ is false, so the $*$ need not be refined

26

further. Thus the dependence test returns two direction vectors: $(<,>)$ and $(=,<)$. Combining these with the execution ordering direction vectors between $S_1$ and $S_2$ (recall that $S_1 \; \Theta_{(\leq, *)} \; S_2$ and $S_2 \; \Theta_{(\leq, *, \neq)} \; S_1$) we get the dependence relations:

$$S_1 \; \delta_{(=, <)} \; S_2 \qquad \text{and} \qquad S_1 \; \delta_{(<, >)} \; S_2$$

**Unknown Loop Limits.** One advantage of Banerjee's inequalities is that in many actual cases, some of the terms will drop out altogether [Alle83]. For instance, the $(A_k - B_k) L_k$ term that appears in many of the bounds will be zero when $A_k = B_k$, which is common. Some $LB_k$ or $UB_k$ do not depend on the either loop limit for certain directions when $A_k = B_k$; for instance, in the example above, the bound $UB_k^<$ is independent of the loop limits. If all the $LB_k$ or all the $UB_k$ can be found without knowing some of the loop limits, then one of the sums $\sum_{k=1}^{d} LB_k$ or $\sum_{k=1}^{d} UB_k$ can be computed and tested against $B_0 - A_0$.

    *Example.* Take the previous example and replace the loop limits by unknown variables:

```
        do I = 1, N
           do J = 1, M
S₁:           A(I*10+J) = ...
S₂:           ... = A(I*10+J-1)
           enddo
        enddo
```

Now the values of some of the $LB$ and $UB$ depend on the unknown variables:

$$
\begin{array}{llll}
LB_I^* = -10N+10 & LB_I^< = -10N+10 & LB_I^= = 0 & LB_I^> = 10 \\
UB_I^* = 10N-10 & UB_I^< = -10 & UB_I^= = 0 & UB_I^> = 10N-10 \\
LB_J^* = -M+1 & LB_J^< = -M+1 & LB_J^= = 0 & LB_J^> = 1 \\
UB_J^* = M-1 & UB_J^< = -1 & UB_J^= = 0 & UB_J^> = M-1
\end{array}
$$

Filling in the dependence hierarchy with just the known values gives the dependence hierarchy shown below:

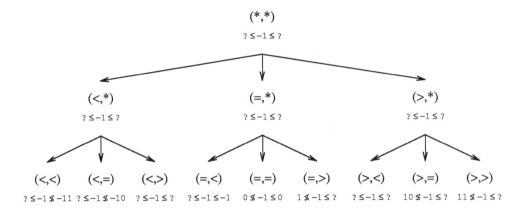

We are left with the three direction vectors: $(<,>)$, $(=,<)$ and $(>,<)$. Thus, the computed dependence relations are:

$$S_1 \; \delta_{(<,>)} \; S_2, \; S_1 \; \delta_{(=,<)} \; S_2, \; S_2 \; \overline{\delta}_{(<,>)} \; S_1.$$

Symbolic analysis could be used to determine if some simple run-time test would eliminate a dependence. For instance, the actual equations for the $(>,<)$ direction are:

$$-M+11 \; \leq \; -1 \; \leq \; 10N-11$$

Rearrangement gives the condition $M \geq 12$; if this condition is false, there is no dependence with that direction.

In general, the GCD test and Banerjee's inequalities present necessary but not sufficient conditions for dependence. Whenever the loop limits are known and the coefficients $A_k$ and $B_k$ all satisfy:

$$A_k, \; B_k \in \{ \; C, \; 0, \; -C \; \}$$

for some integer constant $C$, then the test is exact.

### 2.5.3 Exact Algorithm for a Single Loop Index

Banerjee also created another data dependence decision algorithm which not only gives necessary and sufficient conditions for dependence, but in fact can enumerate the iterations involved in the dependence relation. Most cases can be handled with this simple version of the algorithm since most subscripts involve only a single loop index variable. Here we have modified Banerjee's algorithm again to handle direction vector tests. This exact algorithm makes use of the following lemma [Kirc74]:

Let $a$, $b$, and $k$ be integers such that $a$ and $b$ are not both zero, and let $g = \mathrm{GCD}(a, b)$. If $x = x^1$, $y = y^1$ is any solution to the equation

$$ax - by = k$$

then all solutions to this equation are given by

$$x = x^1 + tb/g, \quad y = y^1 + ta/g$$

where $t$ can take any integral value.

Kirch also gives an efficient algorithm to find both the $g = \text{GCD}(a, b)$, and one solution to the equation $ax - by = \text{GCD}(a, b)$, which we reproduce in Program 2.1.

---

**Program 2.1.** Kirch's algorithm.

```
procedure FINDGCD (A,B; var G,X,Y);
  if A = 0 and B = 0 then
    G = 0; X = 0; Y = 0;
  else if A = 0 then
    G = ABS(B); X = 0; Y = -B/G;
  else if B = 0 then
    G = ABS(A); X = A/G; Y = 0;
  else /* first, initialize */
    A0 = 1; A1 = 0; B0 = 0; B1 = 1; G0 = ABS(A); G1 = ABS(B);
    Q = G0 / G1; R = G0 mod G1;
    while R ≠ 0 loop
      A2 = A0 - Q * A1; A0 = A1; A1 = A2;
      B2 = B0 - Q * B1; B0 = B1; B1 = B2;
      G0 = G1; G1 = R;
      Q = G0 / G1; R = G0 mod G1;
    endloop;
    G = G1; X = A1; Y = -B1;
    if A < 0 then
      X = -X;
    endif
    if B < 0 then
      Y = -Y;
    endif
  endif
end FINDGCD;
```

---

**The Algorithm.** Let us now explain the exact algorithm. Because it deals with only a single loop index variable, the subscript functions $f$ and $g$ must be defined as:

$$f(I_1,...,I_d) = A_0 + A_m I_m$$
$$g(I_1,...,I_d) = B_0 + B_m I_m.$$

and $\psi_m$ is the direction vector element to be tested. We assume that either $A_m \neq 0$ or $B_m \neq 0$.

1) Let $g = \text{GCD}(A_m, B_m)$ and let $(x^0, y^0)$ be any solution to the equation

$$A_m x^0 - B_m y^0 = g.$$

2) If $g$ does not divide $B_0 - A_0$, then there is no dependence (by the GCD test).
3) Let $x^1 = x^0(B_0 - A_0)/g$ and $y^1 = y^0(B_0 - A_0)/g$.
   So $(x^1, y^1)$ is a solution to the equation

$$A_m x - B_m y = (B_0 - A_0).$$

By Kirch's Lemma, all solutions to this equation are given by

$$x = x^1 + tB_m/g, \ y = y^1 + tA_m/g.$$

where $t$ is any integer.

4) We will derive conditions which must be met for dependence to exist by looking at the following known relations for $x$ and $y$.

$$x \geq L_m \qquad x \leq U_m \qquad x \ \psi_m \ y \qquad y \geq L_m \qquad y \leq U_m$$

where $\psi_m$ is the $m^{\text{th}}$ element of the direction vector. From these, we derive bounds on t as follows:

$x \geq L_m$

$$x^1 + tB_m/g \geq L_m$$

$$t \geq (L_m - x^1)(g/B_m), \ \text{if } B_m > 0 \tag{L1}$$

$$t \leq (L_m - x^1)(g/B_m), \ \text{if } B_m < 0 \tag{U1}$$

$$x^1 \geq L_m, \ \text{if } B_m = 0 \tag{T1}$$

$x \leq U_m$

$$x^1 + tB_m/g \leq U_m$$

$$t \leq (U_m - x^1)(g/B_m), \ \text{if } B_m > 0 \tag{U2}$$

$$t \geq (U_m - x^1)(g/B_m), \ \text{if } B_m < 0 \tag{L2}$$

$$x^1 \leq U_m, \ \text{if } B_m = 0 \tag{T2}$$

$y \geq L_m$

$$y^1 + tA_m/g \geq L_m$$

$$t \geq (L_m - y^1)(g/A_m), \ \text{if } A_m > 0 \tag{L3}$$

$$t \leq (L_m - y^1)(g/A_m), \ \text{if } A_m < 0 \tag{U3}$$

$$y^1 \geq L_m, \ \text{if } A_m = 0 \tag{T3}$$

$$y \leq U_m$$

$$y^1 + tA_m/g \leq U_m$$

$$t \leq (U_m - y^1) (g/A_m), \text{ if } A_m > 0 \quad \text{(U4)}$$

$$t \geq (U_m - y^1) (g/A_m), \text{ if } A_m < 0 \quad \text{(L4)}$$

$$y^1 \leq U_m, \text{ if } A_m = 0 \quad \text{(T4)}$$

x $\psi_m$ y

This is divided into several cases dependent on the value of $\psi_m$. If $\psi_m \equiv *$, then no additional constraints can be determined.

$\psi_m \equiv <$

$$x < y$$

$$x \leq y - 1$$

$$x^1 + tB_m/g \leq y^1 + tA_m/g - 1$$

$$t (B_m - A_m)/g \leq y^1 - x^1 - 1$$

$$t \leq (y^1 - x^1 - 1) g/ (B_m - A_m), \text{ if } B_m > A_m \quad \text{(U5)}$$

$$t \geq (y^1 - x^1 - 1) g/ (B_m - A_m), \text{ if } B_m < A_m \quad \text{(L5)}$$

$$x^1 \leq y^1 - 1, \text{ if } B_m = A_m \quad \text{(T5)}$$

$\psi_m \equiv =$

$$x = y$$

$$x^1 + tB_m/g = y^1 + tA_m/g$$

$$t (B_m - A_m)/g = y^1 - x^1$$

$$t = (y^1 - x^1) g/ (B_m - A_m), \text{ if } B_m \neq A_m \quad \text{(L6,U6)}$$

$$x^1 = y^1, \text{ if } B_m = A_m \quad \text{(T6)}$$

$\psi_m \equiv >$

$$x > y$$

$$x^1 + tB_m/g \geq y^1 + tA_m/g + 1$$

$$t (B_m - A_m)/g \geq y^1 - x^1 + 1$$

$$t \geq (y^1 - x^1 + 1) g/ (B_m - A_m), \text{ if } B_m > A_m \quad \text{(L7)}$$

$$t \leq (y^1 - x^1 + 1) g/ (B_m - A_m), \text{ if } B_m < A_m \quad \text{(U7)}$$

$$x^1 \geq y^1 + 1, \text{ if } B_m = A_m \quad \text{(T7)}$$

Now, by using the appropriate relations above, we should have a lower bound $t_L$ on t (the maximum bound from L1-L7), an upper bound $t_U$ on t from (the minimum bound from U1-U7), and perhaps some truth tests which must be satisfied for the dependence relation to exist. If the appropriate T1-T7 are not satisfied by $x^1$ and $y^1$, or if $t_U < t_L$, then there is no dependence relation with that direction. If the conditions and bounds constraints are satisfied, then we can derive values of $x$ and $y$ which cause dependence from the bounds of $t$ and the equations in step 5; therefore we can prove by example that dependence does exist. A program to implement this algorithm is shown in Programs 2.2 and 2.3.

The Exact Algorithm only works exactly when the loop increment is one; when the increment is not one, the normalized loop indices $\bar{I}^n$ and the functions $f^n$ and $g^n$ should be used if possible. When the loop lower limit is unknown, $f^n$ and $g^n$ will be unsuitable unless

---

**Program 2.2.** Program to compute dependence with exact test.

```
integer TL, TU;
boolean INDEPENDENT;

procedure EXACT ( A0, B0, AM, BM, LM, UM, ψ );
    /* INDEPENDENT will be set TRUE if no data dependence relation */
    TL = -∞;  TU = ∞;
    FINDGCD ( AM, BM, G, X, Y );
    if (B0-A0) mod G ≠ 0 then
        INDEPENDENT = TRUE;
    else
        X = X * ( B0 - A0 ) / G;
        Y = Y * ( B0 - A0 ) / G;
        INDEPENDENT = FALSE;
        TEST ( BM/G, LM-X );
        TEST ( -BM/G, X-UM );
        TEST ( AM/G, LM-Y );
        TEST ( -AM/G, Y-UM );
        case ψ
        of "*" then /* do nothing */
        of "<" then
            TEST ( AM-BM, X-Y+1 );
        of "=" then /* simulate = by using both >= and <= */
            TEST ( AM-BM, X-Y );
            TEST ( BM-AM, Y-X );
        of ">" then
            TEST ( BM-AM, Y-X+1 );
        endcase;
        if TU < TL then
            INDEPENDENT = TRUE;
        endif;
    endif;
end EXACT;
```

---

**Program 2.3.** TEST subroutine used in Program 2.2.

```
procedure TEST ( TMUL, RHS );
    /* inequality was t*TMUL >= RHS */
    if TMUL = 0 then
        if RHS > 0 then
            INDEPENDENT = TRUE;
        endif;
    else if TMUL > 0 then
        TL = max ( TL, RHS / TMUL );
    else
        TU = min ( TU, RHS / TMUL );
    endif;
    return TRUE;
end TEST;
```

$A_m = B_m$, as the loop lower limit $L_m$ will appear as an unknown value in the constant expression. Even in these rare cases, this algorithm will give a conservative but inexact answer by ignoring the increment, assuming that it is one.

*Example.* The exact algorithm applied to the loop:

```
        do I = 1,10
S₁:        X(I+10) = ...
S₂:        ... = X(2*I+1)
        enddo
```

begins by finding $GCD (2, 1) = 1$, and a solution to

$$1x - 2y = 1 = GCD (2, 1).$$

One such solution is:

$$x^0 = 1, \quad y^0 = 0.$$

Then a solution is found to the dependence equation

$$1x - 2y = 1 - 10 = B_0 - A_0.$$

This solution is

$$x^1 = -9, \quad y^1 = 0.$$

All solutions to the dependence equation are given by

$$x = -9 + 2t, \quad y = t.$$

From the conditions in step (4) we get the following bounds on the free variable $t$:

(L1)  $t \geq 5$
(U2)  $t \leq 9$
(L3)  $t \geq 1$
(U4)  $t \leq 10$

Since only the extrema need be saved, we have $5 \leq t \leq 9$. For the direction of $(<)$, the additional relation

(U5)  $t \leq 8$

is added; this gives a range of $5 \leq t \leq 8$ for a $(<)$ direction, which corresponds to the data dependence relations:

$S_1[1] \; \delta \; S_2[5]$
$S_1[3] \; \delta \; S_2[6]$
$S_1[5] \; \delta \; S_2[7]$
$S_1[6] \; \delta \; S_2[8]$

all of which clearly have a $(<)$ direction vector. For the direction of $(=)$, the additional relation

(L6,U6)  $t = 9$

is computed, which corresponds to the data dependence:

$S_1[9] \; \delta \; S_2[9]$

The direction of $(>)$ gives the relation

(L7)  $t \geq 10$

which is incompatible with the previously computed range of $t$, so there is no intersection with the $(>)$ direction vector.

Notice that the same algorithm could be used to test for dependence for two distinct indices, such as:

```
do I = 1, 100
  do J = 2, 50
    A(I) = ...
    ... = A(J)
  enddo
enddo
```

The modifications to the algorithm would be to handle different upper and lower limits for $x$ and $y$; the direction vector element would be treated like a $*$ (since the direction vector does not test for a relation between $I$ and $J$).

## 2.5.4 Exact Algorithm for Multiple Indices

Neither Banerjee's equations nor the Exact Algorithm will satisfactorily compute dependence in triangular loops, such as in Figure 2.4.

---

```
do I = 1, 100
    do J = 1, I-1
        A(I*100+J) = A(J*100+I)
    enddo
enddo
```

**Figure 2.4.** Triangular loop example.

---

We describe here a generalization of the Exact Algorithm from the previous section to handle multiple loop index variables. For simplicity, assume that all loops have an increment of one. This algorithm will find $2d$-1 free variables $(t_1, ..., t_{2d-1})$, and will put bounds on these variables derived from the loop limits and the direction vector. The bounds will be in terms of the loop limits and other free variables. The algorithm has the distinct disadvantage that it requires time $O(2^{2d-1})$, exponential in the number of free variables.

**First step.** Remember that the dependence equation is:

$$\sum_{k=1}^{d} (A_k i_k - B_k j_k) = B_0 - A_0$$

Introduce a change of variables:

$$C_0 = B_0 - A_0$$
$$C_{2k-1} = A_k, \quad C_{2k} = -B_k, \quad \text{for } 1 \le k \le d$$
$$h_{2k-1} = i_k, \quad h_{2k} = j_k, \quad \text{for } 1 \le k \le d$$

The dependence equation is now equivalent to:

$$\sum_{k=1}^{2d} C_k h_k = C_0$$

The rest of the algorithm will find $2d-1$ free variables, $t_1$ to $t_{2d-1}$, and will define each $h_k$ in terms of these, as:

$$h_k = S_{k,0} + \sum_{n=1}^{k} S_{k,n} t_n, \quad \text{for } 1 \le k \le 2d-1$$

The definition for $h_{2d}$ will be the same, except there is no $t_{2d}$ (or we could equivalently define $t_{2d}=0$).

**Second step.** Let $E_{2d-1} = -C_{2d}$ and let $p_{2d-1} \equiv h_{2d}$; notice that $E_{2d-1}$ is an actual integer constant to this algorithm, while $p_{2d-1}$ is an unknown variable for which we are solving. Execute the following for $m = 2d-1, 2d-2, ..., 2$:

*Reduction:*

The dependence equation is equivalent to:

$$\sum_{k=1}^{m-1} C_k h_k + C_m h_m - E_m p_m = C_0$$

Find $E_{m-1} = \mathrm{GCD}(C_m, E_m)$ and a solution $(X_m^0, Y_m^0)$ to the equation $C_m X - E_m Y = E_{m-1}$. Replace the term $C_m h_m - E_m p_m$ by $E_{m-1} p_{m-1}$, where

$$p_{m-1} \equiv C_m h_m / E_{m-1} - E_m p_m / E_{m-1}$$

to get the dependence equation to look like:

$$\sum_{k=1}^{m-1} C_k h_k - E_{m-1} p_{m-1} = C_0$$

This completes the induction for the next iteration.
The reduction step completes with an equation

$$C_1 h_1 - E_1 p_1 = C_0$$

**Third step.** Solve the final equation from the reduction step as in the single variable exact test; equivalently, the reduction step could be carried one more iteration to find $E_0 = \mathrm{GCD}(C_1, E_1)$, and a solution $(X_1^0, Y_1^0)$ to $C_1 X - E_1 Y = E_0$. By the GCD test, if $E_0$ does not divide $C_0$, then these references are independent. Otherwise, compute

$$X_1^1 = X_1^0 * C_0 / E_0, \quad Y_1^1 = Y_1^0 * C_0 / E_0$$

to give $C_1 X_1^1 - E_1 Y_1^1 = C_0$. By Kirch's Lemma, all solutions are given by:

$$X_1 = X_1^1 + t_1 E_1 / E_0, \quad Y_1 = Y_1^1 + t_1 C_1 / E_0$$

Notice that $X_1$ is in fact $h_1$, so we have found

$$h_1 = S_{1,0} + S_{1,1} t_1$$

for $S_{1,0} = X_1^1$, $S_{1,1} = E_1 / E_0$. Also notice that $Y_1$ is really $p_1$; for use in the next step, define $R_{1,0} = Y_1^1$, $R_{1,1} = C_1 / E_0$.

**Fourth step.** Execute the following for $m = 2, ..., 2d-1$:

*Substitution:*

We start with

$$h_k = S_{k,0} + \sum_{n=1}^{k} S_{k,n} t_n, \quad \text{for } 1 \leq k \leq m-1$$

$$p_{m-1} = R_{m-1,0} + \sum_{n=1}^{m-1} R_{m-1,n}$$

Recall that $p_{m-1}$ was defined as

$$C_m h_m / E_{m-1} - E_m p_m / E_{m-1} = p_{m-1} \tag{P}$$

Note that GCD $(C_m / E_{m-1}, E_m / E_{m-1}) = 1$, and we already have a solution $(X_m^0, Y_m^0)$ to the equation $(C_m / E_{m-1}) X - (E_m / E_{m-1}) Y = 1$. Since 1 obviously divides any integer, we symbolically solve for (P) by multiplying through by $p_{m-1}$; so one solution $(X_m^1, Y_m^1)$ to (P) is:

$$X_m^1 = X_m^0 p_{m-1}, \quad Y_m^1 = Y_m^0 p_{m-1}$$

Furthermore, all solutions to (P) are given by:

$$X_m = X_m^0 p_{m-1} + t_m E_m / E_{m-1}, \quad Y_m = Y_m^0 p_{m-1} + t_m C_m / E_{m-1}$$

But, we already have $p_{m-1}$ in terms of $t_1, \ldots, t_{m-1}$. Notice here that $X_m$ is really $h_m$. So, we let

$$S_{m,n} = X_m^0 R_{m-1,n}, \quad 0 \le n \le m-1$$

$$S_{m,m} = E_m / E_{m-1}$$

Similarly, $Y_m$ is really $p_m$; so we let

$$R_{m,n} = Y_m^0 R_{m-1,n}, \quad 0 \le n \le m-1$$

$$R_{m,m} = C_m / E_{m-1}$$

This completes the induction for the next iteration.

**Fifth step.** We finish the fourth step with

$$P_{2d-1} = R_{2d-1,0} + \sum_{n=1}^{2d-1} R_{2d-1,n}$$

Because $p_{2d-1}$ was defined as $h_{2d}$, we can set

$$S_{2d,n} = R_{2d-1,n}, \quad \text{for} \, 1 \le n \le 2d-1$$

Now we have all the loop index variables defined in terms of the free variables:

$$h_k = S_{k,0} + \sum_{n=1}^{k} S_{k,n} t_n, \quad \text{for } 1 \le k \le 2d$$

Here, we have defined $t_{2d} = 0$ and $S_{2d,2d} = 0$, as explained earlier. So far, the complexity of the algorithm has been linear in the number of loops considered.

**Sixth step.** Here we take into account the loop limits. We assume that we know $L_k \le h_k \le U_k$, for all k. In addition, we assume that each $L_k$ or $U_k$ is either unknown, or known and of the form:

$$L_k = L_{k,0} + \sum_{m=1}^{k-1} L_{k,m} h_m$$

37

and likewise for $U_k$. We account for the loop limits by calculating:

$$h_k \geq L_k$$

$$S_{k,0} + \sum_{n=1}^{k} S_{k,n} t_n \geq L_{k,0} + \sum_{m=1}^{k-1} L_{k,m} \left( S_{m,0} + \sum_{n=1}^{m} S_{m,n} t_n \right)$$

$$S_{k,0} + \sum_{n=1}^{k} S_{k,n} t_n \geq L_{k,0} + \sum_{m=1}^{k-1} L_{k,m} S_{m,0} + \sum_{n=1}^{k-1} \sum_{m=n}^{k-1} L_{k,m} S_{m,n} t_n$$

$$S_{k,k} t_k \geq L_{k,0} - S_{k,0} + \sum_{m=1}^{k-1} L_{k,m} S_{m,0} + \sum_{n=1}^{k-1} t_n \left( -S_{k,n} + \sum_{m=n}^{k-1} L_{k,m} S_{m,n} \right)$$

This gives a bound on $t_k$ (if $S_{k,k}$ is not zero), either in terms of other $t$ variables, or a constant bound if (as often happens) all the multipliers turn out to be zero. This will be a lower bound for $t_k$ if $S_{k,k} > 0$, and an upper bound otherwise. If $S_{k,k}$ turns out to be zero, then this inequality can be solved for some $t_j$, where $j$ is the largest integer such that $S_{k,j} \neq 0$. This bounds computation should be carried out for all the known bounds.

**Seventh step.** Here we account for the direction vector. For each direction vector element that is not a "*", we derive a relation:

$$h_{2m-1} \; \psi_m \; h_{2m}$$

Similar to the loop limit calculation, we get:

$$S_{2m-1,0} + \sum_{n=1}^{2m-1} S_{2m-1,n} t_n \; \psi_m \; S_{2m,0} + \sum_{n=1}^{2m} S_{2m,n} t_n$$

$$S_{2m,2m} t_{2m} \; \psi_m^{-1} \; S_{2m-1,0} - S_{2m,0} + \sum_{n=1}^{2m-1} t_n \left( S_{2m-1,n} - S_{2m,n} \right)$$

Again, this gives a bound on $t_{2m}$, either in terms of other $t$ variables or a constant bound. Whether this is a lower or upper bound depends on the sign of $S_{2m,2m}$ and the direction vector element $\psi_m$. Note that if a direction of "<" is being tested, then the right hand side of this inequality should be incremented by one to change to a non-strict inequality, and decremented by one for ">". If $S_{2m,2m}$ is zero, then this inequality should be solved for $t_j$, as in the sixth step.

**Eighth step.** This is the exponential step. We have $t_1$ through $t_{2d-1}$, each with a (possibly empty) list of lower and upper bounds:

$$T_{k,0}^L + \sum_{n=1}^{k-1} T_{k,n}^L t_n \leq t_k \leq T_{k,0}^U + \sum_{n=1}^{k-1} T_{k,n}^U t_n$$

The $t$ variables define a space with $2d-1$ dimensions. The bounds we have calculated for the $t$ variables define a convex hull in this space; if this convex hull is actually empty, then we can prove independence. We try to prove this by comparing the least upper bound to the greatest lower bound for a $t_1$. Note that the bounds for $t_1$ must be constants, if they are known at all. If the range for $t_1$ is empty, then the array references are independent. If the range is not empty, then we look at the bounds of $t_2$ at the lower and at the upper bounds of $t_1$. If the range for $t_2$ is empty at *both* bounds of $t_1$, then we have independence. If either range is not empty, then we look at the bounds of $t_3$ at each of the four upper/lower bounds combinations of $t_1$ and $t_2$, and so on.

If dependence is being computed for statements $S_v$ and $S_w$ that are nested in $d_v$ and $d_w$ loops, then there will be additional index variables in the computation (with associated loop limits), but no additional direction vector elements. Programs 2.4-2.10 at the end of this chapter implement this algorithm.

*Example.* To compute the dependence relations for the loop in Figure 2.4, we start out with the following:

$$C_4 = -100$$
$$C_3 = 1$$
$$C_2 = -1$$
$$C_1 = 100$$
$$C_0 = 0$$

The reduction step computes the following:

| m | $C_m$ | $E_m$ | $E_{m-1}$ | $X_m$ | $Y_m$ |
|---|---|---|---|---|---|
| 3 | 1 | 100 | 1 | 1 | 0 |
| 2 | -1 | 1 | 1 | -1 | 0 |
| 1 | 100 | 1 | 1 | 0 | 1 |

Since $E_0$ is one, the GCD test fails; the substitution step defines the index variables in terms of the free variables:

$$h_1 = i_1 = t_1$$
$$h_2 = j_1 = t_2$$
$$h_3 = i_2 = 100t_3 - t_2 + 100t_1$$
$$h_4 = j_2 = t_3$$

After enforcing the loop limits, the bounds on the free variables are:

$$1 \le t_1 \le 100$$
$$1 \le t_2 \le 100$$
$$t_2 + 100t_1 + 1 \le 100t_3 \le 101t_1 + t_2 - 1$$
$$1 \le t_3 \le t_2 - 1$$

At first, we look at the (*,*) direction vector. We find this table of bounds for the free variables:

$$1 \leq t_1 \leq 100$$

| $t_1 = 1$ | | $t_1 = 100$ | |
| $1 \leq t_2 \leq 100$ | | $1 \leq t_2 \leq 100$ | |
|---|---|---|---|
| $t_2 = 1$ | $t_2 = 100$ | $t_2 = 1$ | $t_2 = 100$ |
| $2 \leq t_3 \leq 0$ | $3 \leq t_3 \leq 2$ | $101 \leq t_3 \leq 0$ | $102 \leq t_3 \leq -102$ |

Because all of the bounds at the bottom of the table are inconsistent, these two array references must be completely independent.

## 2.6 Unknown Variables

We have already seen examples with unknown loop limits. If there is an unknown integer variable in the subscript, that variable can be treated just like another loop index variable for which no lower or upper limits are known [Wall88]. This has value even in the simple GCD test:

```
do I = 1, 10
   A(I*2-1) = ...
   ... = A(I*2-N*4)
enddo
```

Many dependence algorithms would give up at the appearance of the unknown variable N in the subscript and assume the worst case. But the GCD test can treat N as just another variable without limits, since it doesn't inspect the limits anyway. In this case, GCD(2,2,4)=2, which does not divide the difference of 1.

**Assertions.** In some instances, the compiler may be able to symbolically perform dependence testing in such a way as to ask the user a question about the program. In the program:

```
do I = 1, 10
   A(I+N) = ...
   ... = A(I)
enddo
```

if we treat N as just another loop index variable (with lower and upper bounds of N), then we can use Banerjee's Inequalities to find the limits:

$$LB_I^* = -9 \quad LB_I^< = -9 \quad LB_I^= = 0 \quad LB_I^> = 1$$
$$UB_I^* = 9 \quad UB_I^< = -1 \quad UB_I^= = 0 \quad UB_I^> = 9$$
$$LB_N^* = N$$
$$UB_N^* = N$$

This gives the inequality:

$$N-9 \le 0 \le N+9$$

for dependence with the $(*)$ direction in the $I$ loop. From this, we can see that if $N < -9$ or $N > 9$, then there is no dependence. To test for the $(<)$ direction, we get the inequality:

$$N-9 \le 0 \le N-1$$

meaning that if $N \le 0$ or $N \ge 10$, then there is no $\delta_{(<)}^*$ relation. This symbolic information can be used to query the user interactively, or to prompt for assertions that can be inserted into the program [Elli85].

## 2.7 Linearization of Multidimensional Arrays

There has been some discussion in the literature about how to perform data dependence testing of multidimensional arrays. Early work in data dependence side-stepped the problem by suggesting that all arrays should be "linearized," that is, converted to single dimensioned arrays by mapping the subscripts. Thus:

```
real A(10,10)
A(I,J) = ...
```

would become

```
real A(100)
A(I+J*100-100) = ...
```

Unfortunately, the Exact Algorithm for a single index does not apply when linearization introduces multiple loop indices in a single subscript; also, Banerjee's equations, which would be exact in a subscript-by-subscript test above, become less precise when the coefficients differ, as happens with linearization. The following loop shows how linearization can reduce the precision of dependence testing:

```
        real X(10,10)
        do I = 1,5
            do J = 1,5
S₁:             X(I,2*J) = ...
S₂:             ... = X(I,J)
            enddo
        enddo
```

has the dependence relation $S_1 \; \delta_{(=,<)} \; S_2$ as computed by Banerjee's equations. Linearization changes this to

```
        real X(100)
        do I = 1,5
            do J = 1,5
S₁:             X(I+20*J-10) = ...
S₂:             ... = X(I+10*J-10)
            enddo
        enddo
```

Here, Banerjee's equations find intersection with a direction vector of $(*,<)$, which results in the dependences: $S_1 \; \delta_{(\leq,<)} \; S_2$ and $S_2 \; \overline{\delta}_{(<,=)} \; S_1$.

There are counterexamples where subscript-by-subscript testing fails. Testing each subscript individually in the loop:

```
        real X(10,10)
        do I = 1,5
S₁:         X(I+1,I+2) = ...
S₂:         ... = X(I,I)
        enddo
```

gives the dependence relation $S_1 \; \delta_{(<)} \; S_2$. Linearization gives the loop:

```
        real X(100)
        do I = 1,5
S₁:         X(11*I+11) = ...
S₂:         ... = X(11*I-10)
        enddo
```

which has no dependence by the GCD test.

Even the GCD test does not always benefit from linearization, however, as seen in the loop:

```
      real X(7,7)
      do I = 1,3
          do J = 1,3
S₁:           X(2*I+1,2*J+1) = ...
S₂:               ... = X(2*I,2*J)
          enddo
      enddo
```

which has no intersection in either subscript by the GCD test. Linearization, however, produces the loop:

```
      real X(49)
      do I = 1,3
          do J = 1,3
S₁:           X(2*I+14*J+1) = ...
S₂:               ... = X(2*I+14*J-7)
          enddo
      enddo
```

In the linearized case, the GCD test fails, although Banerjee's equations correctly compute no dependence.

Neither the GCD test nor Banerjee's equations uniformly improves with linearization. In those cases when a loop index variable is used in more than one subscript, linearizing (perhaps just those subscripts) can improve the GCD test and the Exact Algorithm.

Some cases require linearization, however. The subscript-by-subscript test assumes that subscript bounds are not violated. Linearization of array references is the only way to find dependences due to violation of array bounds. In Fortran programs, EQUIVALENCE statements can map arrays onto each other such that the only way to compute dependence is to linearize the references:

```
      real A(10,10),B(5,20)
      equivalence (A,B)
```

In the Fortran standard, multiple aliasing through parameters or COMMON is allowed only when none of the aliases are defined. Thus:

```
common X(100),Y(100)
real A(100)
call SUB(X,A(1),A(2))
end
subroutine SUB(D,E,F)
real D(10,10),E(100),F(99)
common X(100),Y(100)
D(1,1) = ...
E(2) = F(2)
end
```

is nonstandard Fortran, since D and X are aliases for the same memory locations, as are E and F. Most languages do not have this restriction, and most Fortran implementations allow multiple aliasing. In these cases, linearizing all array references and even mapping all arrays to a global array MEM is necessary [BuCy86].

On the other hand, there are cases where linearization is impossible. The Fortran 8X proposed standard allows for allocatable arrays and array sections:

```
real,array(:,:),allocatable:: A
allocate A(1:100,1:100)
call SUB(A(1:100:2,99:1:-1))
end
subroutine SUB(B)
real,array(:,:):: B
B(1,2) = 10
end
```

The array A cannot be linearized since it may be allocated with different bounds in different executions of the program. The array B cannot be linearized since the bounds are different on different calls.

Thus the issue of linearization is a complex one. We suggest that the best approach is to perform dependence testing subscript-by-subscript generally; where possible, the GCD test can also be performed on the linearized array.

## 2.8 Additional Complications

Here we investigate some of the complications in dependence testing in real programs. One often forgotten aspect of dependence testing in academic presentations is the dependence of Input or Output statements upon each other. Certainly, the order in which lines are read or written to a file is important; this implies that there is a dependence from each **read** or **write** statement to each other that might refer to the same file. If the compiler can prove that two statements read from different files, then there may be no dependence between them. Other IO operations, such as rewinding a file, also must fit into the dependence graph.

Sometimes there needs to be dependence between **read**s and **write**s, even if they look like they deal with different files. For example, some operating systems allow a user to redirect input or output from multiple logical files to the same physical file, meaning that there are multiple output paths to the same file. What looks to the program like different files may be the same file; in this environment, the compiler must take the conservative approach and assume that all files can overlap. Another example is when the **write** statement is writing a prompt to the user asking for the next line of input. In that case, the compiler must insert a dependences, so that the prompt comes out at the proper time.

When dealing with library subroutines, there may be some unknown side-effects. Some of the side-effects may be assignments to global variables other than the formal parameters of the program, or IO operations. These global variables may not be visible to the program being compiled; to be conservative, compilers must assume that all calls to unknown subroutines must be performed in the same order as the original program.

One unique case occurs with **volatile** variables. A **volatile** variable is one whose value may change without explicit actions taken by the program. These are often added to a programming language to allow a program to refer to system variables or device registers through memory locations. The device registers are updated asynchronously by the hardware; to properly deal with **volatile** variables, the compiler must not try to keep these variables in registers, for instance. In particular, the order of fetches from a **volatile** variable may be important. This is one case where data input-dependence does truly make sense. For instance, the Digital Equipment Corporation PDP-8 had a small number of memory locations that incremented themselves each time they were referenced. Obviously, the order of the fetches to those locations is important.

## 2.9 Comparison with other methods

There has been much work in the area of computing dependence graphs. Some of this work was done in developing vectorizing compilers for the many vector and parallel supercomputers and mini-supercomputers in the market today. Many of the modern compilers use techniques similar to those described here. There are stronger data dependence testing methods, but these have some disadvantages with compared with this work.

**Ad Hoc Methods.** When developing Fortran compilers for the Cray-1 and the CDC Cyber 205, the manufacturers had to develop special optimizing compilers that would discover operations that could be done in vector mode on the target machine. Since there was no vector language in wide use (and Fortran 8x is only now becoming available), these optimizations had to discover vector operations in serial **do** loops. The prime concern was to preserve the results. A second concern is to find vector operations without additional human input; users do not want to have to rewrite their programs when they get a new machine. The compiler had to be able to discover, from the source program, whether or not a loop could safely be vectorized. Thus, the compiler had to find data dependence relations within the program.

The methods used in the CFT compiler available from Cray Research [Cray86] and the FTN200 compiler from Control Data [CoDa84] are relatively weak when compared to the direction vector method. Generally, the strategy used is to look for constructs that might prevent vectorization of a loop; these constructs range from IF statements in the loop to presence of arithmetic recurrences. Another construct that prevents vectorization is an array subscript that is too complicated; only a few subscript forms are allowed. For example, CFT only vectorizes simple subscripts of the form:

$$\pm \text{ invariant } * \text{ index-variable} \pm \text{ invariant.}$$

Only a single subscript is allowed to vary in the loop; all other subscripts must be invariant (diagonal array references are not vectorized).

Also, these compilers look only at the innermost loop; if that loop did not vectorize (in its entirety), then those statements were executed serially. This is taken up again in Chapters 3 and 6.

**Banerjee.** In his early work, Banerjee derived a subscript test that was generally applicable to most common subscript forms [Bane76]. This test was a binary test; it told only YES or NO, if there could or could not be a dependence. The work done here has modified this test to give more information in a direction vector.

In his Ph.D. thesis, Banerjee derived an exact subscript test for subscripts that contain a single index variable. This test returns the entire index set for which dependence exists, which gives complete knowledge about the dependence. The work done here has again modified this test to compress the information returned by the test into a direction vector, rather than saving the complete index set.

**Kuhn.** In his Ph.D. thesis, Kuhn derived an exact method of computing data dependence, called Data Arc Sets [Kuhn80]. This method accepted a less general form of subscripts than Banerjee's method, however it produced much more information. The output was not only a binary YES/NO, but the domain and range of the dependence in the iteration space. This method gives much more information than direction vectors, but requires more time to compute and more space to store the information. Many transformations do not need the extra information provided by Data Arc Sets (as shown in Chapters 3 through 6), although some transformation can use exact information (such as the wavefront method, see Chapter 8). Another strength of Data Arc Sets is that it has the capability of using "covering" information. When one assignment to a variable A occurs between an earlier assignment and a later use, the middle assignment may "cover" the data flow-dependence from the earlier assignment and the later use. This was shown earlier for scalars; a similar example would work for arrays. While it is more powerful, it takes more time and space and can accept less general subscript forms than the direction vector method described here. The Data Arc Set method might be more fruitfully applied in a less general way, such as finding exact dependence for small parts of loops that show problems when considered only by a simpler method.

46

**Allen and Kennedy.** Allen and Kennedy also modified Banerjee's early test to produce more information than binary dependence [Kenn80, AlKe87]. However, their modification is not as general as direction vectors. Their test tells which **do** loops must be executed serially for this dependence relation to be satisfied. This information in fact can be found from the direction vector attached to the particular data dependence.

If a data dependence direction vector has a forward direction (<) in position k, then there is a dependence from some iteration of the **do** $I_k$ loop, say $i_k$, to some later iteration of that loop. By executing the **do** $I_k$ loop serially we can ensure that iteration $i_k$ is indeed executed before any later iteration of that loop, and that will satisfy the constraints of the data dependence relation. Allen and Kennedy's test will give the nest level of the outermost loop that satisfies this property; in this case it will return k. In general, it will return, for each data dependence relation, the outermost nest level for which the direction vector has a forward direction in that dimension. They call this a *loop dependent* dependence, meaning that the dependence occurs due to the presence of the loop. A *loop independent* dependence corresponds to a dependence with all equal directions.

Allen and Kennedy also give a special test for deciding whether interchanging two loops is legal. As we will show in Chapter 6, interchanging two loops is legal if there are no dependence relations which contain a (<,>) pair in the data dependence direction vector. Allen and Kennedy's test turns out to be equivalent to this requirement. Thus both of their tests are special cases of direction vector tests.

**Heuft and Little.** Heuft and Little [HeLi82] responded to some old results by Banerjee et al [BCKT79] by pointing out that a more precise dependence analysis can produce better program speedup. While the main point of the paper was not that they had more precise dependence analysis methods, they did present another method to look at data dependence relations. Their method turns out to be equivalent to finding the dependence distance in each dimension. As we noticed earlier, the dependence distance is very useful knowledge, but it may not be as simple (in general) as Heuft and Little assume. Finding dependence distances will limit the form of subscripts that can be accepted by the subscript test, and increase the time and space required to compute and save the information.

In addition, Heuft and Little were looking at a special target machine application, the data flow machine architecture. A data flow machine theoretically has more parallelism than current manufactured machines. Thus, a more exact dependence analysis may produce benefits in the cases where it applies. For more mundane machines, this extra information is largely wasted.

**Lamport.** Lamport [Lamp74] described two methods for executing **do** loops in parallel, the Coordinate method and the Hyperplane method. To check the validity of either method, he develops tests based on the array subscripts, which essentially compute the data dependence distance in each loop index variable. However, he only shows how to compute the dependence distance for array references with extremely simple subscripts, with the form:

index-variable ± integer-constant

He states that his results can be generalized. In fact, we can show that his Coordinate method is equivalent to loop vectorization (shown in Chapter 3) and his Hyperplane method is equivalent to the wavefront method for solving recurrences (shown in Chapter 8).

**Wallace.** Wallace [Wall88] describes a new decision algorithm for computing data dependence relations using integer programming. His method can deal with multiple subscripts simultaneously, and he claims it is efficient. It has not yet been modified to compute data dependence direction vectors. More experience with his method is necessary to compare it to other more classical decision algorithms.

## 2.10 Program for Multiple Index Exact Test

In this program, D is the number of loops that surround both statements being tested, while DD is the number of loop index variables being tested, which will be at least 2*D in this program.

---

**Program 2.4.** Exact test for multiple indices.

```
integer D, DD;
array C, E, X, Y, R, Ψ;
array of array S, L, U;
array NTL, NTU; /* number of lower/upper bounds for T */
array of array of array TL, TU;
boolean INDEPENDENT;

procedure MAIN; /* assume C, L, U are already filled in */
   INDEPENDENT = FALSE;
   REDUCTION;
   if C[0] mod E[0] ≠ 0 then
      INDEPENDENT = TRUE;
   else
      SUBSTITUTION;
      ENFORCE_LIMITS;
      ENFORCE_DIRECTION;
      if CHECK_BOUNDS(1) then
         INDEPENDENT = TRUE;
      endif;
   endif;
end MAIN;
```

---

**Program 2.5.** Reduction step for program 2.4.

```
procedure REDUCTION;
   E[DD-1] = -C[DD];
   for M = DD-1 downto 1 loop
      FINDGCD( C[M], E[M], E[M-1], X[M], Y[M] );
   endloop;
end REDUCTION;
```

---

**Program 2.6.** Substitution step for program 2.4.

```
procedure SUBSTITUTION;
  R[0] = C[0]/E[0];
  for M = 1 to DD-1 loop
    for N = 0 to M-1 loop
        S[M,N] = X[M]*R[N];
        R[N] = Y[M]*R[N];
    endloop;
    S[M,M] = E[M] / E[M-1];
    R[M] = C[M] / E[M-1];
  endloop;
  for N = 0 to DD-1 loop
    S[DD,N] = R[N];
  endloop;
  S[DD,DD] = 0;
end SUBSTITUTION;
```

**Program 2.7.** Loop limit step for program 2.4.

```
procedure ENFORCE_LIMITS;
  array V, W;
  for K = 1 to DD loop
    V[0] = S[K,0] - L[K,0];
    W[0] = S[K,0] - U[K,0];
    for M = 1 to K-1 loop
      V[0] = V[0] - L[K,M]*S[M,0];
      W[0] = W[0] - U[K,M]*S[M,0];
    endloop;
    for N = 1 to K-1 loop
      V[N] = S[K,N]; W[N] = S[K,N];
      for M = N to K-1 loop
        V[N] = V[N] - L[K,M]*S[M,N];
        W[N] = W[N] - U[K,M]*S[M,N];
      endloop;
    endloop;
    V[K] = S[K,K];
    W[K] = S[K,K];
    ADDBOUND( V, K, +1 );
    ADDBOUND( W, K, -1 );
  endloop;
end ENFORCE_LIMITS;
```

**Program 2.8.** Reduction step for program 2.4.

```
procedure ENFORCE_DIRECTION;
  array V;
  for M = 1 to D loop
    V[0] = S[2*M,0] - S[2*M-1,0];
    for N = 1 to 2*M-1 loop
      V[N] = S[2*M,N] - S[2*M-1,N];
    endloop;
    V[M] = S[2*M,2*M];
    case Ψ[M]
    of "*" then /* do nothing */
    of "<" then
      V[0] = V[0] - 1;
      ADDBOUND( V, 2*M, +1 );
    of "=" then
      ADDBOUND( V, 2*M, +1 );
      ADDBOUND( V, 2*M, -1 );
    of ">" then
      V[0] = V[0] + 1;
      ADDBOUND( V, 2*M, -1 );
    endcase;
  endloop;
end ENFORCE_DIRECTION;
```

**Program 2.9.** Bounds procedure used in programs 2.7 and 2.8.

```
procedure ADDBOUND ( array V; K, X );
```
/* enforce the relation $\sum_{m=0}^{K} XV_m t_m \geq 0$ */
```
   L = K;
   while V[L] = 0 and L > 0 loop L = L-1 endloop;
   if L = 0 then
      if X*V[0] < 0 then
         INDEPENDENT = TRUE;
      endif;
   else
      if X*V[L] > 0 then /* lower bound on T */
         NTL[L] = NTL[L] + 1;
         N = NTL[L];
         for M = 0 to L-1 loop
            TL[L,N,M] = -X*V[M];
         endloop;
         TL[L,N,L] = X*V[L];
      else /* upper bound on T */
         NTU[L] = NTU[L] + 1; N = NTU[L];
         for M = 0 to L-1 loop
            TU[L,N,M] = -X*V[M];
         endloop;
         TU[L,N,L] = X*V[L];
      endif;
   endif;
end ADDBOUND;
```

**Program 2.10.** Step to check bounds on free variables in program 2.4.

```
array T;

boolean function CHECK_BOUNDS ( K );
   integer XL, XU;
   XL = indef; XU = indef;
   for N = 1 to NTL[K] loop
      X = TL[K,N,0];
      for M = 1 to K-1 loop  /* any computation with indef returns indef */
         X = X + TL[K,N,M] * T[M];  /* except 0*indef returns 0 */
      endloop;
      X = X / TL[K,N,K];
      XL = MAX( XL, X );
   endloop;
   for N = 1 to NTU[K] loop
      X = TU[K,N,0];
      for M = 1 to K-1 loop
         X = X + TU[K,N,M] * T[M];
      endloop;
      X = X / TU[K,N,K];
      XU = MIN( XU, X );
   endloop;
   if XL > XU then
      return TRUE;
   elseif K < DD-1 then
      T[K] = XL;
      if CHECK_BOUNDS( K+1 ) then
         T[K] = XU;
         if CHECK_BOUNDS( K+1 ) then
            return TRUE;
         endif;
      endif;
   endif;
   return FALSE;
end CHECK_BOUNDS;
```

# 3 Vectorization

"Vectorizing compilers" are commonly available from all vendors selling vector supercomputers and mini-supercomputers, such as Cray Research, Convex, Hitachi, Fujitsu, NEC, IBM and so forth. The goal of automatic vectorization is to accept code that was written in a language which was designed for a serial computer (typically a serial **do** loop) and translate it into code which uses the vector instructions of the target machine.

Vectorization is perhaps best shown by a simple example. The simple serial **do** loop:

```
do I = 1, 50
   A(I) = B(I) + C(I)
   D(I) = A(I) / 2.0
enddo
```

can be executed in vector mode; we use the proposed Fortran 8x array assignment syntax [ANSI87] to represent vector operations:

```
A(1:50) = B(1:50) + C(1:50)
D(1:50) = A(1:50) / 2.0
```

This syntax means that elements 1 to 50 of the array B are added to elements 1 to 50 of array C, and the results are stored in elements 1 to 50 of array A. Then these same elements of A are divided by 2 and the results stored in array D. Note that all the additions are computed by the first statement before any divisions are computed by the second statement. Vectorization has replaced the **do** loop control by implicit indexing within each array assignment statement. For a simple memory to memory vector computer (such as the ETA 10), a compiler might generate machine code for this loop like:

```
vadd    A[1], B[1], C[1], 50
vdiv    D[1], A[1], sr9, 50
```

This would stream elements of B and C starting at B[1] and C[1], add the corresponding elements, and store the vector of results back into the array A, with a vector length of 50. The second statement would perform the corresponding divides, using a scalar register presumably already loaded with the value 2.0. Many computers (such as the Cray machines) use vector registers to store intermediate vector results, much as they use scalar registers to hold intermediate scalar results. The corresponding code for such a computer might be:

```
mov        VL, 50
vload          V1, B[1], 1
vload          V2, C[1], 1
vadd       V1, V2, V3
vstore         V3, A[1], 1
vdiv       V3, S1, V4
vstore         V4, D[1], 1
```

The first statement loads the "vector length" register, which is used for all vector instructions. The vload instructions load a vector register from memory, starting at the specified memory address and incrementing through memory with the given stride. The other instructions are self-explanatory, with again a scalar register used in the floating point divide.

If there is a dependence relation in the loop that prevents vectorization, then the compiler can attempt several simple transformations on the loop to remove the problem. When the dependence graph of the loop is acyclic, then statement reordering will always allow vectorization. A topological sort of the dependence graph will tell how to order the statements.

If the graph is cyclic, then the dependence cycles should be studied to see if the cycle can be broken or classified into one of a number of known reduction or recurrence forms. Multi-statement cycles can be handled by using statement substitution to decrease the number of statements involved in the cycle. This method is not always successful, but sometimes the cycle can be reduced until it involves only a single statement.

If a cycle in the graph cannot be reduced to a single statement, then *loop distribution* can be employed to remove the cycle to a separate loop. After loop distribution, the statements involved in the dependence cycle are in one serial loop, and the rest of the vectorized statements will appear above or below the cycle.

If all the statements in a loop are involved in a big dependence cycle, then the compiler can try to split vectorizable expressions out. This involves creating compiler temporary vectors to hold the results of the vectorized subexpressions. A dependence graph based on atoms (single variable references) and operations is necessary to allow the compiler to decide which operations are not involved in the cycle.

Finally, the compiler must not only be able to decide when a loop can be vectorized, but must be able to decide when vectorizing a loop is the proper course of action. In some cases, if only part of the loop can be executed on the machine with vector instructions and the rest of the loop must be executed in serial mode, then the loop can be done faster by executing the whole loop in serial mode. This case occurs when the loop limits are small and vector startup time is large.

This chapter explains the dependence test that is used to vectorize a loop, and tells how to perform transformations to allow vectorization of a loop.

## 3.1 Vectorization Test

A vectorizing compiler must discover when the statements in a loop can be executed with vector instructions. The discovery process can be broken into two parts. First, the compiler must build the dependence graph for the loop and discover any cycles in the graph; if there are no cycles, then the loop can be trivially vectorized. If there are any dependence cycles, the compiler must inspect the cycles to see if they can be broken or classified as one of a known type of reduction or recurrence operation that can be executed with a vector instruction or replaced by a subroutine library call. Second, the compiler must inspect each statement of a vectorizable loop and decide whether the target machine has vector instructions capable of executing that statement.

A sufficient (but not necessary) condition for vectorizing a loop is to have no lexically backward dependence arcs. This is overly restrictive is many cases, though it may be enough of a test for a simple vectorizer. More general cases can be easily handled by using the fast algorithm developed by Tarjan [Tarj72], shown in Program 3.1. This algorithm takes linear time and space with respect to the number of arcs and nodes in the dependence graph. Each maximal cycle in the dependence graph will be identified, either as a multi-statement cycle or a single statement self-cycle. This allows each cycle to be attacked individually to either classify it as a known type of recurrence or to try to break the cycle.

*Example.* The loop below:

```
       do I = 2, N
S₁:        A(I) = B(I) + C(I)
S₂:        D(I) = A(I+1) + 1
S₃:        C(I) = D(I)
       enddo
```

has the dependence relations:

$$S_1 \,\bar{\delta}\, S_3 \qquad S_2 \,\bar{\delta}\, S_1 \qquad S_2 \,\delta\, S_3$$

The data dependence graph can be represented graphically as:

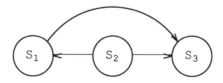

While there is a lexically backward dependence, there are no dependence cycles, so statement reordering will allow simple vectorization. A topological sort of the dependence graph would produce the correct vector code:

**Program 3.1.** Tarjan's algorithm.

```
integer I, P;
procedure FINDCYCLE(V);
    P = P + 1; STACK(P) = V; INSTACK(V) = true;
    I = I + 1; LOWLINK(V) = I; NUMBER(V) = I;
    for W such that S_V δ* S_W do
        if NUMBER(W) = 0 then
            FINDCYCLE(W);
            LOWLINK(V) = min(LOWLINK(V),LOWLINK(W));
        else if NUMBER(W) < NUMBER(V) then
            if INSTACK(W) then
                LOWLINK(V) = min(LOWLINK(V),LOWLINK(W));
            end if;
        end if;
    end for;
    if LOWLINK(V) = NUMBER(V) then
        if STACK(P) = V then
            /* S_V is a self-cycle if S_V δ* S_V */
            /* S_V is a vector operation otherwise */
            P = P - 1; INSTACK(V) = false;
        else /* S_V is in a multi-statement dependence cycle; */
            while NUMBER(STACK(P)) >= NUMBER(V) do
                W = STACK(P); P = P - 1; INSTACK(W) = false;
            end while; /* S_W is part of this dependence cycle; */
        end if;
    end if;
end procedure;

    P = 0; STACK(P) = 0; I = 0;
    INSTACK(*) = false; NUMBER(*) = 0;
    for S = 1 to NUMBER_STATEMENTS do
        if NUMBER(S) = 0 then
            FINDCYCLE(S);
        end if;
    end for;
```

$S_2$: D(2:N) = A(3:N+1) + 1
$S_1$: A(2:N) = B(2:N) + C(2:N)
$S_3$: C(2:N) = D(2:N)

**Reductions.** Many single statement dependence cycles can be recognized as simple reduction operations, such as the finding sum, product, maximum or minimum of a vector. These are called reduction operations because they "reduce" a vector of operands to a single result. Thus, the loop:

```
       do I = 1, N
S₁:       A(I) = B(I) + C(I)
S₂:       S = S + A(I)
S₃:       AMAX = MAX(AMAX,A(I))
       enddo
```

has the dependence graph:

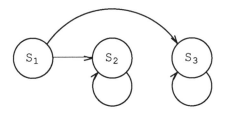

The reductions in statements $S_2$ and $S_3$ show up as cycles in the dependence graph. A compiler would inspect these cycles and recognize the reduction operations; equivalent vector code would be:

```
S₁: A(1:N) = B(1:N) + C(1:N)
S₂: S = S + SUM(A(1:N))
S₃: AMAX = MAX(AMAX,MAXVAL(A(1:N)))
```

**Other Idioms.** Recognizing other idioms is also important for performance. Many single statement operations can be replaced by calls to numerical library routines. Common idioms are:

```
do I = 2, N
    X(I) = A(I) + B(I)*X(I-1)
enddo
```

```
do I = 2, N
    X(I) = A(I) - B(I)*X(I-1)
enddo
```

```
do I = 2, N
    X(I) = A(I)*(B(I) - X(I-1))
enddo
```

## 3.2. Statement Substitution

When the dependence graph for a loop has multi-statement cycles, then no amount of state-ment reordering will allow the loop to be fully vectorized. If the dependence cycle can be reduced to a single statement cycle, then perhaps the cycle can be recognized as one of the spe-cial idioms. This can sometimes be done with statement substitution. A simple statement sub-stitution method is given here that will work in many cases. First let us study the effects of statement substitution.

If we have two assignment statements, $S_v$ and $S_w$, where the left hand side variable of $S_v$ is $X$ and $X$ is used on the right hand side of $S_w$, and $S_v \, \delta \, S_w$, then we may be able to substitute the right hand side expression of $S_v$ for the reference to $X$ in $S_w$. The dependence graph for the modified program will also be changed. First, the dependence relation $S_v \, \delta \, S_w$ will be removed from the dependence graph. Then, relations $S_t \, \delta \, S_w$ will be added for all statements $S_t$ such that $S_t \, \delta \, S_v$ was in the original dependence graph. Similarly, relations $S_w \, \bar{\delta} \, S_x$ will be added for all statements $S_x$ such that $S_v \, \bar{\delta} \, S_x$ was in the original dependence graph.

*Example.* The dependence graph for the statements below:

```
S₁:  A = 1
S₂:  B = A + 2
S₃:  C = 2
S₄:  D = B + C
```

is shown below:

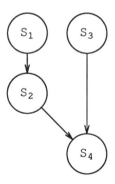

The variable B in statement $S_4$ can be replaced by a copy of the right hand side expression of statement $S_2$, the assignment to B:

```
S₁:  A = 1
S₂:  B = A + 2
S₃:  C = 2
S₄:  D = (A + 2) + C
```

the modified dependence graph is:

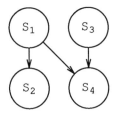

Notice that statement substitution is illegal if it introduces spurious dependence arcs. In the statements below:

$S_1$: A = 1
$S_2$: B = A + 2
$S_3$: A = 2
$S_4$: D = B + C

simple substitution of statement $S_2$ into statement $S_4$ would introduce the dependence $S_3 \, \delta \, S_4$ instead of $S_1 \, \delta \, S_4$; the modified program would compute $D = 5$, while the correct answer is $D = 4$. Lemma 3.1 explains when simple statement substitution is legal.

Lemma 3.1 uses the concept of the dominator relationship [AhSU86]. Statement $S_v$ *dominates* statement $S_w$ if every path from the beginning of the program to $S_w$ goes through $S_v$. By this definition, every statement dominates itself, and the entry point of a loop dominates all statements in the loop. Testing for the dominator relationship is explained in [AhSU86].

**Lemma 3.1**

If assignment statements $S_v$ and $S_w$ are in a loop L, and $S_v \, \delta_{(=)} \, S_w$, then $S_v$ may be substituted into $S_w$ only if

(1) $S_v$ dominates $S_w$, and

(2) there is no statement $S_x$ between $S_v$ and $S_w$ with $S_v \, \overline{\delta}_{(=)} \, S_x$ or $S_v \, \delta^o_{(=)} \, S_x$.

**Proof.**

Suppose X is the left hand side variable of $S_v$.

1) If $S_v \, \overline{\delta}_{(=)} \, S_x$ for some $S_x$, then some variable on the right hand side of $S_v$ (say Y) is reassigned in $S_x$; substituting the right hand side expression of $S_v$ for X in $S_w$ would be illegal since then $S_w$ would get the new value of Y (computed in $S_x$), not the value that was used in $S_v$.

2) If $S_v \, \delta^o_{(=)} \, S_x$ for some $S_x$, then X is reassigned in $S_x$; substituting the right hand side expression of $S_v$ for X in $S_w$ would be illegal since $S_w$ would not get the value of X from $S_x$ as it should, but would use the value of the $S_v$ expression.

3) If $S_v$ does not dominate $S_w$, then substituting the right hand side expression of $S_v$ for X in $S_w$ would be illegal since $S_v$ might not be executed before $S_w$, and $S_w$ would not get the "old" value of X, as it should.

In the loop below, the dependence relation $S_1 \, \delta_{(=)} \, S_3$ holds:

```
        do I = 1, N
S₁:     A(I) = C(I) + B(I)
S₂:     C(I) = E(I)
S₃:     B(I+1) = A(I) + 2
        enddo
```

Statement substitution of $S_1$ into $S_3$ is illegal, however, since $S_1\ \overline{\delta}_{(=)}\ S_2$ also holds. Reordering the statements, however, allows statement substitution:

```
        do I = 1, N
S₁:     A(I) = C(I) + B(I)
S₃:     B(I+1) = (C(I)+B(I)) + 2
S₂:     C(I) = E(I)
        enddo
```

Now, what was a multi-statement data flow-dependence cycle ($S_1\ \delta\ S_3\ \delta\ S_1$) has been reduced to a single statement cycle in $S_3$.

Statement substitution will not always reduce a multi-statement dependence cycle to a single statement cycle. If a loop contains a multi-statement data flow-dependence cycle, and two or more of the statements in the cycle have self-cycles in the dependence graph, then statement substitution will not reduce the dependence cycle to a single statement self-cycle. At best, the cycle can be reduced to include only those statements which have self-cycles.

## 3.3 Partial Vectorization

For loops with unvectorizable dependence cycles, partial vectorization may be useful. Partial vectorization means leaving statements involved in dependence cycles in serial loops while still vectorizing the rest of the loop.

*Example.* The loop below:

```
        do I = 1, 100
S₁:     A(I) = B(I) + C(I)
S₂:     D(I) = A(I) / E(I)
S₃:     E(I+1) = (D(I) + D(I+1)) / 2.0
S₄:     F(I) = SQRT(E(I))
        enddo
```

has the dependence graph:

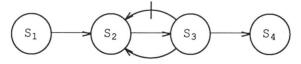

Statements $S_2$ and $S_3$ comprise a dependence cycle. The whole loop cannot be vectorized due to the cycle; however, partial vectorization of $S_1$ and $S_4$ is legal:

```
S₁:  A(1:100) = B(1:100) + C(1:100)
     do I = 1, 100
S₂:     D(I) = A(I) / E(I)
S₃:     E(I+1) = (D(I) + D(I+1)) / 2.0
     enddo
S₄:  F(1:100) = SQRT(E(1:100))
```

One way to do partial vectorization is via $\pi$-partitioning [Towl76]. Each maximal strongly connected component in the dependence graph (as found by Tarjan's algorithm) is treated as a unit, or $\pi$-block. The dependence graph then induces an acyclic partial ordering on the $\pi$-blocks. For the loop above, the $\pi$-blocks are:

$$\pi_1 = \{S_1\} \quad \pi_2 = \{S_2, S_3\} \quad \pi_3 = \{S_4\}$$

and the induced partial ordering is:

Since there is certainly some overhead associated with each serial **do** loop, it is important not to needlessly distribute serial loops. When multiple cycles show up in the dependence graph, it is usually more efficient to try to merge the cycles into a single serial loop.

**Subexpression Vectorization.** Even if all the statements in a loop are involved in a dependence cycle, some vectorization may be possible. Each statement may perform several operations, some which may not be involved in the cycle of dependence. With a more detailed dependence graph, the compiler can find which variables and which operations are involved in the dependence cycle. In all our dependence graphs so far, nodes have represented statements. A more detailed graph would have a node for each operation and operand. Those operations which do not participate in the cycle can be split out; new assignments to copy the results of these operations to compiler temporary variables can be added, and the compiler temporary variable can replace the original operation. Arithmetic laws of commutativity, associativity and distributivity, if they apply, may increase the number of operations that can be split out.

*Example.* In the loop below, all statements are involved in a dependence cycle:

```
     do I = 1, N
S₁:     A(I) = C(I) + E(I)*B(I)
S₂:     B(I) = D + A(I) + G(I)
S₃:     C(I+1) = A(I) + B(I) + F(I)
     enddo
```

as can be seen in the dependence graph:

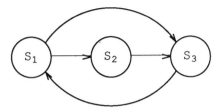

A detailed dependence graph based on the atoms of the loop shows that not all operations participate in the dependence cycle:

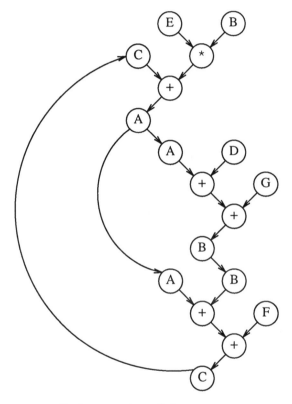

In particular, the "E(I)*B(I)" of $S_1$ can be split into a separate statement and vectorized:

```
        T(1:N)  =  E(1:N)*B(1:N)
        do I = 1,  N
S₁:       A(I)  =  C(I)  +  T(I)
S₂:       B(I)  =  D  +  A(I)  +  G(I)
S₃:       C(I+1)  =  A(I)  +  B(I)  +  F(I)
        enddo
```

By using the laws of commutativity and associativity, $S_2$ can be rewritten to allow the subexpression "D+G(I)" to be vectorized also:

```
        T(1:N)  =  E(1:N)*B(1:N)
        U(1:N)  =  D + G(1:N)
        do I = 1, N
S₁:       A(I) = C(I) + T(I)
S₂:       B(I) = U(I) + A(I)
S₃:       C(I+1) = A(I) + B(I) + F(I)
        enddo
```

There is a certain amount of danger in using the laws of commutativity, associativity and distributivity to transform the order of operations being performed in the program. Roundoff errors due to inexact computer arithmetic will accumulate differently, or unexpected underflow or overflow conditions may creep in. In general, more freedom is allowed in transforming integer expressions.

Adding compiler temporary arrays creates new problems. This issue is discussed in Chapter 9.

## 3.4 Dependence Cycle Breaking

**Ignorable Cycles.** Self-anti-dependence cycles can usually be ignored when vectorizing loops. On most vector computers, the fetches for the right hand side vector operands are guaranteed to complete before vector stores are performed. Thus, any anti-dependence from the right hand side expression to the left hand side variable can be ignored. For instance, the loop:

```
        do I = 1, N
S₁:       A(I) = A(I+1) - 1
        enddo
```

can be vectorized on today's vector computers, even though it exhibits the dependence cycle $S_1 \bar{\delta}_{(<)} S_1$. This presumes that either all right hand side fetches are done before any stores are done, or that all right hand fetches for $I=i$ are done before any stores for $I=j$, $j>i$ are done.

Similarly, sometimes self-output-dependence cycles can be ignored when vectorizing loops. Many vector computers have indexed scatter instructions, allowing vector execution of the loop:

```
        do I = 1, N
S₁:       B(IP(I)) = A(I)
        enddo
```

If the index vector IP has duplicate elements (say IP(1)=IP(3)=5), the indexed scatter

64

works one of two ways. It may be nondeterministic, meaning that the final value stored into $B(5)$ will be one of $A(1)$ or $A(3)$, but the compiler cannot determine which. Usually, however, indexed scatters are deterministic, meaning that the final value of $B(5)$ will be $A(3)$. For machines with deterministic indexed scatters, a loop like the one shown can be automatically vectorized in spite of the dependence cycle $S_1 \, \delta^o_{(<)} \, S_1$.

**Index Set Splitting.** When there is a cycle of data flow-dependence and data anti-dependence, *index set splitting* can be applied. The dependence graph for the loop below:

```
      do I = 1, 100
S₁:      A(I) = B(101-I) + T
S₂:      B(I) = E(I)
      enddo
```

is:

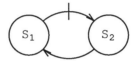

By splitting the index set into disjoint parts, as below, we break the dependence cycle:

```
       do I = 1, 50
S₁ₐ:      A(I) = B(101-I) + T
S₂ₐ:      B(I) = E(I)
       enddo
       do I = 51, 100
S₁ᵦ:      A(I) = B(101-I) + T
S₂ᵦ:      B(I) = E(I)
       enddo
```

The modified dependence graph is acyclic:

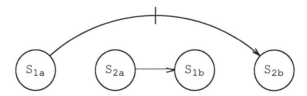

Cases where index set splitting is useful are often characterized by a single pair of array references causing a cycle of dependence, either a flow- and an anti-dependence, or a cycle of output-dependence; the dependence "changes direction" in the middle of the index set. For more information about index set splitting, see [Bane79, AlKe87].

**Node Splitting.** When a dependence cycle includes data flow-dependence and data anti-dependence, as below, *node splitting* can sometimes be applied to break the cycle:

```
       do I = 1, N
S₁:       A(I)   =  (B(I)+B(I+1))/2
S₂:       B(I+1) = E(I)
       enddo
```

The dependence graph for this loop is:

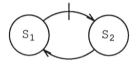

In this case, the cycle appears only because statement nodes are used in the dependence graph. An operator-node graph would not show a cycle.

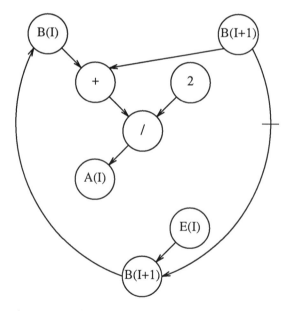

By copying the array B into a compiler temporary, we remove the dependence cycle, and vectorization is possible:

```
S₁ₐ: T(1:N)   =  B(2:N+1)
S₂:  B(2:N+1) =  E(1:N)
S₁ᵦ: A(1:N)   =  (B(1:N)+T(1:N))/2
```

Note that for vector register computers, the added statement corresponds to a vector register load, which must be performed anyway, so this transformation adds no overhead. This is called *node splitting* because it removes a cycle by splitting the node in the dependence graph into two nodes. For more information, see [KKPL81, AlKe87].

**Semantically Null Cycles.** Some dependence cycles may be semantically ignorable. For instance, the loop:

```
        do I = 1, N
S₁:         A(I) = A(5)
        enddo
```

has a real data dependence cycle. Iterations 1-5 read the old value of $A(5)$; then a new value is assigned to $A(5)$, and the remaining iterations use that new value. One way to vectorize this loop is to split the index set into those two parts:

```
S₁ₐ: A(1:5)  = A(5)
S₁ᵦ: A(6:N)  = A(5)
```

However, the slightest semantic reasoning would discover that the new value assigned to $A(5)$ is exactly the same as the old value, and therefore simple vectorization is legal:

```
S₁:  A(1:N)  = A(5)
```

Another example is shown by a cycle of output dependence:

```
        do I = 1, N
            do J = 1, N
S₁:             A(I,J) = 0.
S₂:             A(J+1,I) = 0.
            enddo
        enddo
```

This example was found in a production code. Data dependence testing found a cycle of output dependence linking the two statements. However, since the right hand sides are loop invariant and identical, it doesn't really matter in what order the assignments are done, so the dependence cycle can be ignored:

```
S₁:  A(1:N,1:N)  = 0.
S₂:  A(2:N+1,1:N) = 0.
```

## 3.5 Nested Loop Vectorization

Some vector computers could traverse two-dimensional (Burroughs BSP) or three-dimensional (Texas Instruments ASC) vector operands in a single vector instruction. For machines like this, it is reasonable to try to vectorize more than the inner loop. It may also be desirable to vectorize nested loops just to convert serial algorithms into parallel or vector algorithms.

There are two methods to deal with vectorization of nested structures. Muraoka's original method [Mura71], also called "inside-out" vectorization, started by vectorizing the innermost loops. Each array assignment or serial π-block in the inner loop is then treated as a node in the dependence graph for the next outer loop. This next outer loop is vectorized, and the process is repeated until the whole loop nest is visited. Thus, the loop nest:

```
      do I = 1, N
        do J = 1, N
S₁:         A(I,J) = B(I,J) + C(I,J)
S₂:         B(I+1,J) = A(I,J) + 2
S₃:         D(I,J) = D(I,J) + 2
        enddo
      enddo
```

would be vectorized by looking at the dependence graph for the inner loop first:

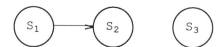

Since there are no cycles, the inner loop can be vectorized:

```
      do I = 1, N
S₁:     A(I,1:N) = B(I,1:N) + C(I,1:N)
S₂:     B(I+1,1:N) = A(I,1:N) + 2
S₃:     D(I,1:N) = D(I,1:N) + 2
      enddo
```

Then, the dependence graph for the outer loop is inspected:

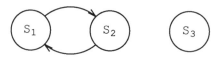

The dependence cycle involving $S_1$ and $S_2$ must be left serial, but $S_3$ can be vectorized for the second loop:

```
      do I = 1, N
S₁:     A(I,1:N) = B(I,1:N) + C(I,1:N)
S₂:     B(I+1,1:N) = A(I,1:N) + 2
      enddo
S₃: D(1:N,1:N) = D(1:N,1:N) + 2
```

An alternate method, used in PFC [AlKe87] and early Parafrase work, is called "outside-in" vectorization. This method starts by building a dependence graph for the whole loop nest. Any statements that do not participate in a dependence cycle can be vectorized for all the loops at once. Dependence cycles are handled by "freezing the outer loop", that is, by distributing the outer loop around the π-block, and vectorizing the next inner loop for that π-block. With this method, the original loop above would be vectorized first by looking at the dependence graph for the outer loop (also shown above). The statements in the cycle would be left in a

68

serial loop, but since $S_3$ is completely independent, it can be immediately vectorized in all loops:

```
        do I = 1, N
            do J = 1, N
S₁:             A(I,J) = B(I,J) + C(I,J)
S₂:             B(I+1,J) = A(I,J) + 2
            enddo
        enddo
S₃:   D(1:N,1:N) = D(1:N,1:N) + 2
```

Now, the **do** I loop is "frozen", that is, dependence relations carried by this loop (with a "<" in the direction vector for this loop) are ignored. The dependence graph for the **do** J loop is inspected:

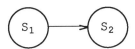

Since there are no cycles, this loop can be vectorized:

```
        do I = 1, N
S₁:       A(I,1:N) = B(I,1:N) + C(I,1:N)
S₂:       B(I+1,1:N) = A(I,1:N) + 2
        enddo
S₃:   D(1:N,1:N) = D(1:N,1:N) + 2
```

The two methods end with the same result if both are taken to the limit. The advantage of inside-out vectorization is that it can stop easily after vectorizing some limited number of loops. The advantage of outside-in vectorization is that statements which can be vectorized for all loops need not be reconsidered each time. Both of these algorithms were implemented in the Parafrase software. As a practical matter, neither method is much used today in compilers, since current vector computers support only a single vector dimension. Vectorization of nested loops is useful if the loops can be collapsed (the loop limits match the array bounds, meaning that the nested loops can be treated as a single long vector operation).

## 3.6 IFs in Loops

Vectorizing loops containing **if** statements is also important. Most vector computers have some mechanism to execute conditional vector code. Early vectorizing compilers, such as those from Cray and CDC, would not vectorize loops containing **if**s, and thus suffered a great loss of usability. As mentioned in Chapter 2, control dependence is used in a dependence graph to reflect the conditional execution of the statements under control of the **if**. With this abstraction, vectorization can proceed as before, with the control dependence arcs being treated like data dependence arcs in Tarjan's algorithm; again, if there are no dependence cycles, the loop can be vectorized. If the **if** statement appears in a dependence cycle, then the loop will likely be at least partially serial; this is discussed further in Chapter 7.

This does not mean that it will necessarily be simple to generate vector code. The following loop:

```
        do I = 1, N
S₁:        A(I)  =  D(I)  + 1
S₂:        if( B(I) > 0 ) then
S₃:            C(I)  =  C(I)  + A(I)
S₄:            D(I+1) = D(I+1) + 1
        endif
        enddo
```

has an acyclic dependence graph:

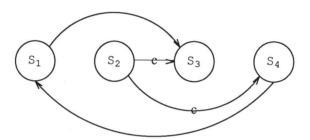

Generation of vector code requires splitting up the conditional block of code:

```
        do I = 1, N
S₂:        temp(1:N)  =  B(1:N)  > 0
S₄:        where ( temp(1:N) ) D(2:N+1) = D(2:N+1) + 1
S₁:        A(1:N)  =  D(1:N)  + 1
S₃:        where ( temp(1:N) ) C(1:N)  =  C(1:N)  + A(1:N)
```

Some compilers may be restricted to generating code for a conditional block of code all at once, in which case the dependence graph would appear to have a dependence cycle involving $S_1$ and the conditional code in $S_2$ and $S_3$, preventing vectorization.

Vectorizing conditional code has other pitfalls. One method of executing conditional vector code is the *controlled store* approach; this is available on many vector computers, such as the Cyber 205 (and its successor, the ETA 10) and the Cray computers. On the Cyber 205, when a controlled store operation is performed, all the operands are fetched from the memory, all the operations are performed, but only those results for which the control vector is set to '1' (or '0') are actually stored into memory. Any faults (such as overflow, etc.) generated for elements that would not be stored are suppressed. The Cray computers have a similar method of operation; a controlled store operation is performed by fetching all the operands into vector registers, performing all the operations, then merging the result vector with the original values of the result array, and storing that. Note that additional vector load operations may be required to get the original values of the result array into a vector register in the first place. Also, there is no way to suppress invalid faults without suppressing all faults, even those that should be detected.

Notice that in both cases, the controlled store vector code executes all iterations of the loop. If the condition is rather sparse, meaning that most of the time the scalar program branches around the conditional code, then the vectorized code may take longer to execute, since it will spend much of its time computing results which it doesn't store. In this case, *compressing* the vector operands is beneficial. For instance, the loop:

```
do I = 1, N
   if( A(I) > 0 ) then
       B(I) = (A(I)*A(I) + B(I)*B(I))*0.5+X
   endif
enddo
```

if vectorized using controlled store operations, would give 6 vector operations of length N. If N1 is the number of '1' bits in the control vector (notice that N1 ≤ N), then compressing the vector operands will allow the conditional vector operations to be performed with a vector length of N1:

```
CV(1:N)  = A(1:N) > 0
TA(1:N1) = PACK( A(1:N), CV(1:N) )
TB(1:N1) = PACK( B(1:N), CV(1:N) )
TB(1:N1) = (TA(1:N1)*TA(1:N1) + TB(1:N1)*TB(1:N1))*0.5+X
B(1:N)   = UNPACK( TB(1:N1), CV(1:N) )
```

If PACK and UNPACK take time proportional to the length of the control vector (as is the case on the Cyber 205), this code has 4 vector operations of length N and 5 vector operations of length N1. The important points to consider are the density of the control vector, the vector length, and the number of vector operands that need to be compressed or decompressed.

A variation of this method is to use indexed gather and scatter operations instead of compress and decompress operations:

```
CV(1:N)  = A(1:N) > 0
TI(1:N1) = PACK( [1:N], CV(1:N) )
TA(1:N1) = A(TI(1:N1))
TB(1:N1) = B(TI(1:N1))
TB(1:N1) = (TA(1:N1)*TA(1:N1) + TB(1:N1)*TB(1:N1))*0.5+X
B(TI(1:N1)) = TB(1:N1)
```

This code has the advantage that there are only two operations with the full vector length (the compare and the PACK), while all the data gathering and arithmetic operations are performed with short vectors. On the Cyber 205 series, the indexed gather and scatter instructions are available, but are significantly slower than compresses or arithmetic operations, making this variation beneficial only when the control vector is very sparse. This code sequence is also available on late model Cray X-MP machines, where the indexed gather corresponds to an indexed vector register load; since the vector register must be loaded anyway, there is little additional overhead associated with this coding sequence.

# 4 Concurrentization

For shared-memory multiprocessor computers, the iterations of the loop can be spread across the processors by having different processors execute different iterations [Sequ87, Alli86]. We use the **doacross** and **doall** statements to represent loops that will be so executed. We use the term *concurrentization* to refer to the process of translating serial loops into code for execution on multiprocessors. It is also sometimes called "parallelization" in the literature.

Actually, any loop can be executed concurrently if the proper synchronizations are added. In the worst case, there will be a synchronization from the bottom of one iteration to the top of the next iteration, resulting in essentially serial execution. Automatic concurrent loop detection is partly a problem of eliminating unnecessary synchronizations, but is also optimizing the loop to reduce the effect of any required synchronizations, and deciding how to schedule the loop on the processors to get the best performance.

## 4.1 Concurrent Loop Scheduling

One approach to *schedule* the iterations of a loop onto processors is the **doacross**, where processor $P_1$ executes the first iteration, $P_2$ executes the second iteration, and so on, until the processors have been exhausted. When the number of iterations exceeds the number of processors (as is often the case with current shared memory multiprocessors), the iterations are folded around the processors. This can be accomplished dynamically by using *self-scheduling,* where each processor executes a critical section to find the next available iteration:

```
enter critical section
global_I = global_I + 1
I = global_I
exit critical section
if I > N then exit
```

Alternatively, the iterations can be preassigned by the compiler, using *prescheduling,* by having each processor execute the loop:

> **do** I = $p$, N, *numberP*

where $p$ is the processor number and *numberP* is the number of processors participating in this concurrent loop.

Another type of concurrent loop is a **doall**; in a **doall**, the iterations may be scheduled on the processors in any order. A processor in a **doall** may execute all consecutive iterations by prescheduling each processor with the loop:

> **do** I = (N/*numberP*) * ($p$−1)+1, (N/*numberP*) *$p$

Another way to schedule a **doall** is to preschedule the iterations in *chunks:*

*enter critical section*
```
global_I = global_I + chunk
local_I = global_I
```
*exit critical section*
```
do I = local_I, MIN(N, local_I+chunk)
```

A **doacross** is used when synchronization between iterations is needed, while a **doall** allows the compiler more flexibility in code generation. Since self-scheduling requires a critical section, it is somewhat more expensive than prescheduling. Prescheduling is well suited for small loops, where the overhead associated with a critical section would dominate. Self-scheduling is well suited for loops containing **if**s and subroutine **call**s, where each iteration may have a different execution time and load balancing is important. Chunking can reduce the impact of the self-scheduling critical section. *Guided self-scheduling,* due to Polychronopoulos [PoKu87] is a tuned type of dynamic chunking that reduces the impact of the critical section, while also reducing the effect of having to wait for one straggling processor to finish the last chunk. Guided self-scheduling works by starting with a large chunk, then scheduling progressively smaller chunks, so the processors have a good chance of finishing at the same time. Each chunk is defined to be $\left\lceil \dfrac{Nleft}{numberP} \right\rceil$, where `Nleft` is the number of iterations that have not yet been scheduled. Several experiments show that guided self scheduling shows remarkably stable performance characteristics over a wide range of applications and machines.

## 4.2 Concurrent Loop Detection

It is easy to show that when all the dependence relations in a loop nest have an equal direction for one loop, that loop can be executed concurrently with no synchronization between the iterations. The equal direction means that there is no data dependence from one iteration of that loop to another iteration of that loop, so there is no need for processors executing different iterations of the loop to communicate data. As with vectorization, any dependence relations with a forward direction in an outer loop will be satisfied by the serial execution of the outer loop.

    *Example.* The dependence relations for the loop below:

```
        do I = 2, N
          do J = 2, N
S₁:          A(I,J) = B(I,J) + 2
S₂:          B(I,J) = A(I-1,J-1) - B(I,J)
          enddo
        enddo
```

are:

$$S_1 \; \delta_{(<,\,<)} \; S_2 \qquad S_1 \; \overline{\delta}_{(=,\,=)} \; S_2$$

Serial execution of the outer I loop will satisfy the flow dependence, and the anti-dependence has an equal direction in both loops, so the J loop can be executed in concurrent mode. In this case, the loops can also be interchanged; then if the J loop is left serial, the I loop can be executed concurrently.

**Concurrent Reductions.** As with vectorization, it is very important to recognize reduction operations and translate these into efficient code for a multiprocessor. A common method is to accumulate partial reductions on each processor, then to combine the partial results at the end of the loop. Thus, for the loop:

```
do I = 1, N
    A(I) = B(I) + C(I)
    S = S + A(I)
enddo
```

each processor might execute the code:

```
SX(p) = 0
do I = p, N, numberP
    A(I) = B(I) + C(I)
    SX(p) = SX(p) + A(I)
enddo
```

then accumulate the partial sums from SX into S at the end of the loop.

## 4.3 Synchronization

Any dependence relation with a non-equal direction that is not part of a reduction must be explicitly satisfied. As with vectorization, some dependences may be broken, reducing the number of dependences that must be handled. In addition, loop alignment and code replication [Padu79, AlKe85, AlCK87] can eliminate dependences that cross iterations.

To satisfy those dependences that can't be removed, synchronization between the processors executing different iterations must be added. There are several types of synchronization primitive [MiPa86, MiPa87]; the choice depends on the target machine's architecture. We survey four types of synchronization here: random synchronization, critical sections, pipelining and barriers.

```
       do I = 2, N
S₁:       A(I) = B(I) + C(I-1)
S₂:       D(I) = A(I) * 2.
S₃:       C(I) = A(I-1) + C(I)
S₄:       E(I) = D(I) + C(I-2)
       enddo
```

**Figure 4.1. Sample loop for concurrentization.**

**Random Synchronization.** The data dependence graph for the loop in Figure 4.1 is shown below:

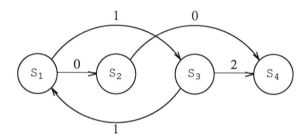

The numbers shown the dependence distance in iterations. This loop can be executed concurrently by adding a synchronization for each dependence with a forward direction:

```
       doacross I = 2, N
          wait (CSYNC, I-1)
S₁:       A(I) = B(I) + C(I-1)
          post (ASYNC, I)
S₂:       D(I) = A(I) * 2.
          wait (ASYNC, I-1)
S₃:       C(I) = A(I-1) + C(I)
          post (CSYNC, I)
          wait (CSYNC, I-2)
S₄:       E(I) = D(I) + C(I-2)
       enddo
```

The speedup for this loop is very small, since S₁[i+1] cannot proceed until S₃[i] has completed. Also, five synchronization primitives were added even to get that 25% overlap.

Two methods to improve the speedup are to reorder the statements and to eliminate unnecessary synchronizations [MiPa86, MiPa87]. Statement reordering can improve the overlap to 50%:

```
      doacross I = 2, N
          wait (CSYNC, I-1)
S₁:       A(I) = B(I) + C(I-1)
          post (ASYNC, I)
          wait (ASYNC, I-1)
S₃:       C(I) = A(I-1) + C(I)
          post (CSYNC, I)
S₂:       D(I) = A(I) * 2.
          wait (CSYNC, I-2)
S₄:       E(I) = D(I) + C(I-2)
      enddo
```

Now, only half of the previous iteration has to complete for another iteration to start execution.

We define the relation $S_v[i] \ll S_w[j]$ to mean that $S_v[i]$ will execute before $S_w[j]$, either because $i=j$ and $S_v$ occurs before $S_w$ in the loop, or due to the synchronization primitives. Note that $\ll$ is transitive. In the above example,

$$S_1[i] \ll S_3[i] \ll S_1[i+1] \ll S_3[i+1],$$

due to the synchronization of the CSYNC variable. This implies that $S_1[i] \ll S_3[i+1]$ without the ASYNC variable. Likewise,

$$S_3[i] \ll S_1[i+1] \ll S_3[i+1] \ll S_1[i+2] \ll S_4[i+2]$$

implies that $S_3[i] \ll S_4[i+2]$ without the **wait** before $S_4$. The improved code would be:

```
      doacross I = 2, N
          wait (CSYNC, I-1)
S₁:       A(I) = B(I) + C(I-1)
S₃:       C(I) = A(I-1) + C(I)
          post (CSYNC, I)
S₂:       D(I) = A(I) * 2.
S₄:       E(I) = D(I) + C(I-2)
      enddo
```

Random synchronization placement is flexible but may require many synchronization points. If these are implemented with a scarce resource, such as a synchronization register, then several dependences may have to be folded into a single synchronization, reducing the potential speedup.

The compiler must also ensure that a conditional synchronization will be satisfied for each iteration. For instance, in the loop:

```
       do I = 2, N
          if ( B(I) > 0 ) then
S₁:          A(I) = A(I) + B(I)
S₂:          C(I) = A(I-1) / 2
          endif
       enddo
```

$S_1$ assigns an element of A that is used by the next iteration of $S_2$. Even though the assignment is conditional, the **post** must be executed on each iteration (even in the assignment is not done), to prevent starvation of the next iteration of $S_2$. One way to do this is to float the **post** below the conditional:

```
       doacross I = 2, N
          if ( B(I) > 0 ) then
S₁:          A(I) = A(I) + B(I)
             wait ( ASYNC, I-1 )
S₂:          C(I) = A(I-1) / 2
          endif
          post ( ASYNC, I )
       enddo
```

Another is to add a dummy **else** clause to perform the posting:

```
       doacross I = 2, N
          if ( B(I) > 0 ) then
S₁:          A(I) = A(I) + B(I)
             post ( ASYNC, I )
             wait ( ASYNC, I-1 )
S₂:          C(I) = A(I-1) / 2
          else
             post ( ASYNC, I )
          endif
       enddo
```

The second approach allows the most potential overlap. Some implementations of synchronization require each **post** operation to be consumed. In that case, a conditional **wait** operation needs to be either floated up above the conditional, or duplicated on the **else** clause also.

**Critical Sections.** A more restricted synchronization strategy is to insert critical sections in the concurrent loop. Any dependence in a loop can be satisfied by a critical section, though in the worst case the critical section will enclose the whole body of the loop.

*Example.* The concurrent loop below has a data dependence cycle from statement $S_1$ to itself; this dependence is satisfied by putting $S_1$ in a critical section.

```
        doacross I = 2,N
            begin critical section
S₁:         A(I) = A(I-1) * B(I) + C(I)
            end critical section
S₂:         C(I) = A(I) + C(I)
S₃:         D(I) = A(I) * 2.
S₄:         E(I) = D(I) + C(I)
        end  doacross
```

The processors execute $S_1$ one at a time, in order, and then go on to execute the rest of the loop independently.

There are two types of critical section. An ordered critical section (used in the example above) requires that iteration I execute the critical section before iteration I+1; thus it acts somewhat like a pipelining segment. In an unordered critical section (more akin to critical sections in operating systems) the order of execution does not matter, as long as only a single processor can execute the code in the critical section at a time. This type of critical section might be useful when accumulating sums in a loop where the order of the summation does not matter. However, as was shown earlier, if the order of the accumulation does not matter then each processor can accumulate a private partial sum; all the partial sums can be combined at the bottom of the loop. Thus the unordered critical section is not very useful; for this reason we use only ordered critical sections here.

The goal is to insert as few critical sections as necessary and especially to make them as small as possible, since the speedup is limited by the size of the largest critical section. Generally speaking, only those statements or operations involved in a data dependence cycle need to be enclosed in a critical section.

Critical sections can provide as much parallelism as random synchronization for lexically backward dependences. The code below shows how the loop in Figure 4.1 can be concurrentized with critical sections:

```
        doacross I = 1,N
            begin critical section
S₁:         A(I) = B(I) + C(I-1)
S₃:         C(I) = A(I-1) + C(I)
            end critical section
S₂:         D(I) = A(I) * 2.
S₄:         E(I) = D(I) + C(I-2)
        end  doacross
```

The **post** and **wait** primitives used in random synchronization essentially enforce a critical section around statements $S_1$ and $S_3$, so the two methods give identical results here. When there are lexically forward dependences, an empty critical section can be used. Notice that some lexically forward dependences may be "covered" by backward dependences that are satisfied by a critical section, as was shown with random synchronization.

**Pipelining.** Another restricted synchronization scheme is pipelining. In the pipelining strategy, a **do** loop is divided into segments of code which are overlapped as in a pipelined arithmetic unit. The segments are created so that the sink of each data dependence relation (that crosses iterations) is either in the same pipeline segment or is in a lexically later segment as the source of that relation. The largest such segment is used as a model for the desired size of all segments; the goal is to make the execution time of all segments roughly the same.

*Example.* In the loop below, the data dependence relation from $S_2$ to $S_1$ means that $S_2$ and $S_1$ must be in the same pipeline segment; thus a segment size of 2 statements is chosen, and the loop is divided into three segments, as shown:

$$\textbf{doacross I = 1, N}$$

$seg\ 1{:}S_1:$     A(I) = B(I) + C(I-1)
$seg\ 1{:}S_2:$     C(I) = A(I-1) + C(I)

$seg\ 2{:}S_3:$     D(I) = A(I) * 2.
$seg\ 2{:}S_4:$     E(I) = D(I) + C(I-2)

$seg\ 3{:}S_5:$     F(I) = E(I) + F(I)
$seg\ 3{:}S_6:$     G(I) = SQRT(F(I)**2 + D(I)**2)
**end doacross**

The execution of the loop is controlled so that execution of segment $s$ for iteration I=i will finish before execution of the same segment for any subsequent iteration. The execution profile for this code is shown below:

Each segment is an ordered critical section; the speedup is limited by the number of segments and the size of the largest segment. Any data dependence cycles must be in a single segment.

Pipelining has the advantage over random synchronization that the number of synchronization points is controlled. However, pipelining will unnecessarily break code that need not be synchronized into separate segments, in order to increase overlap execution for different iterations, adding synchronization overhead. In the above example, there is no reason to synchronize between statements $S_4$ and $S_5$; however, without this segment breakpoint, there would be only two segments and a maximum overlap of two. Another disadvantage is that if all statements are involved in a data dependence cycle, pipelining will serialize the loop by requiring the whole loop to be in the same segment, even though some overlap is possible with random synchronization. Even when no lexically backward dependences appear, pipelining will still limit the amount of parallelism that can be executed.

Previous descriptions of **do** loop pipelining assigned processors to the segments instead of to iterations [PaKL80]. The two formulations are essentially the same.

**Barriers.** The most restricted synchronization strategy is barrier synchronization. This strategy handles only lexically forward dependences. In this strategy, the loop is divided into segments (as in pipelining), but all iterations must complete execution of a segment before execution of the next segment (for any iteration) is started.

*Example.* The loop below can be executed in concurrent mode by using barrier synchronizations:

```
      doall I = 1,N
S₁:       A(I) = B(I)**2
          barrier
S₂:       C(I) = A(I-1) + C(I)
S₃:       D(I) = A(I) * 2.
          barrier
S₄:       E(I) = D(I) + C(I-2)
S₅:       F(I) = E(I) + F(I)
S₆:       G(I) = SQRT(F(I)**2 + D(I)**2)
      end doall
```

The compiler has some flexibility in the placement of the barriers; the dependence from $S_2$ to $S_4$ requires a synchronization, but it can be placed either before or after statement $S_3$. If several barriers can be moved together, they can be merged, thus reducing the total number of barriers. If there are no dependence cycles, statement reordering can change lexically backward dependences into lexically forward dependences, allowing the use of barriers. Barriers are essentially equivalent to loop distribution.

When the only dependence relations are lexically forward in a loop, the use of barrier synchronizations will allow more parallelism than pipelining. Since barriers allow concurrent execution of different iterations of the same segment, perfectly parallel execution is possible. The speedup of pipelining is limited by the number of segments, while the speedup of barrier synchronization is limited by the number of processors or iterations.

Compared to random synchronization, a barrier is like a **post**(SYNC,I) followed immediately by a **wait**(SYNC,[1:N]); random synchronization allows more parallelism because the **wait** is more specific about what iterations need to be completed, and because some independent code can be placed between the **post** and the **wait**. With the barrier, any processor reaching the barrier must wait for all processors to reach that point.

A useful variant of the barrier is a *toll gate* synchronization that allows a processor to proceed when all *previous* iterations (instead of all iterations) reach the toll gate. This is somewhat similar to the pipelining, except again the potential speedup available using toll gate synchronization is limited only by the number of iterations or processors, since different iterations of the same segment can be executed concurrently. It is especially suitable for use by compilers that detect parallelism in serial loops, since all data dependence relations in a serial loop stay in the same iteration, or go to later iterations (there is never a dependence from an iteration to an earlier iteration).

Note that even a toll gate does not provide all the potential parallelism even when only lexically forward dependences are present. For example, concurrent execution of the loop:

```
         do I = 1,N
S₁:         A(I) = B(I) + C(I)*2
S₂:         D(I) = A(I)**2 / D(I)
S₃:         E(I) = (2*D(I) + A(I-1)) * 4
         enddo
```

requires synchronization to satisfy the data communication from $S_1$ to $S_3$ (we assume for this example that loop alignment is not used). Random synchronization, such as:

```
         doacross I = 1,N
S₁:         A(I) = B(I) + C(I)*2
            post(ASYNC,I)
S₂:         D(I) = A(I)**2 / D(I)
            wait(ASYNC,I-1)
S₃:         E(I) = (2*D(I) + A(I-1)) * 4
         enddo
```

allows some iterations to run ahead to $S_2$ before the previous iteration finishes $S_1$, since the **wait** is after the **post**. However, a toll gate is equivalent to moving the **wait**(ASYNC,I-1) to immediately before the **post**(ASYNC,I). A toll gate can be placed anywhere after $S_1$ and before $S_3$, but it strictly orders the processors, which may reduce some actual execution speed, although the theoretical speedup is the same.

**Local Variables.** A compiler that translates serial loops into concurrent loops will recognize the need for such iteration-local variables in the same way that vectorizing compilers promote scalars to arrays [Wolf78]. With most synchronization schemes, if the number of iterations exceeds the number of processors, a processor can complete execution of an entire iteration before picking up a new iteration. The space for the iteration-local temporary variables can be allocated once for each processor and reused for each iteration executed by that processor. The local variables could be allocated in processor registers or in local memory.

When barrier synchronization (or loop distribution) is used, however, this flexibility is not available. The concurrent loop below uses a temporary variable T; the declaration of the temporary T inside the concurrent loop means that each iteration is to use its own copy of the variable.

```
         doall I = 1,N
            real T
S₁:         T = A(I) + B(I)*2
S₂:         C(I) = T**2 / D(I)
            barrier
S₃:         E(I) = (2*C(I) + C(I-1) + C(I+1)) / T
         enddo
```

With barrier synchronization, when the number of iterations exceeds the number of processors, a processor can complete only a segment of an iteration before it must start that segment for another iteration; thus, the iteration-local variables for all iterations must be allocated for the whole loop. This can waste memory and can also reduce optimization possibilities, since the iteration-local variables must be allocated in memory (they cannot be assigned to processor registers), requiring memory stores and loads. Toll gate barriers are sufficiently flexible to solve this complaint about barriers.

## 4.4 Nested Concurrent Loops

Detection of nested concurrent loops is no problem; if all dependences have equal directions in two or more loops, then all the loops can be executed concurrently:

```
doall I = 1, N
    doall J = 1, M
        do K = 1, P
            A(I,J) = A(I,J) + B(I,K)*C(K,J)
        enddo
    enddo
enddo
```

Generation of code for nested concurrent loops may not be so simple. We study two simple paradigms here.

**Loop Coalescing.** Just as nested vector loops can be collapsed to treat the nested loops as a single long vector, nested concurrent loops can be *coalesced* to treat them like a single loop [Poly87]. In this way, the loop above would be translated into:

```
doall IJ = 0, N*M-1
    I = IJ / M + 1
    J = IJ mod M + 1
    do K = 1, P
        A(I,J) = A(I,J) + B(I,K)*C(K,J)
    enddo
enddo
```

This obviates the need for dealing with nested concurrent loops at all.

**Nested Concurrency.** A more general approach is to handle nested concurrent loops directly. This allows, for instance, a concurrent loop to call a subroutine, where the subroutine can also have more concurrent loops. There are certain requirements on the implementation to handle general nested concurrency. Some sort of cactus stack arrangement must be used, so that each concurrent iteration will have its own local variables and can have its own stack of activation records for subroutine calls. A Cactus stack should allow each subroutine to refer to any global variables or parameters from the calling routine. Also, some mechanism must be used to schedule the processors over the multiple levels of concurrency. The processors can be statically assigned over the nested concurrent loops [PoKP86, Cytr87], or use some sort of dynamic scheduling technique, such as a global task queue.

## 4.5 Synchronization Implementation

The most primitive synchronization primitives are **post** and **wait** (or **set** and **test** [MiPa86, MiPa87]). Most other synchronization paradigms can be implemented in terms of **post** and **wait**.

---

```
        event ASYNC
        doacross I = 1, N
S₁:       A(I+1) = B(I) + C(I)
          post ( ASYNC, I )
S₂:       D(I) = A(I+1) / 2
          wait ( ASYNC, I-1 )
S₃:       C(I) = A(I)
        enddo
```

**Figure 4.2.** Sample **doacross** loop.

---

In Figure 4.2, the dependence from $S_1$ to $S_3$ is synchronized using a synchronization variable, ASYNC. Notice that the distance of the dependence is explicit (1). There are three obvious methods to implement this type of synchronization. We shall show that they differ greatly in the time spent initializing the synchronization variable and in the sequencing required by the scheme.

The first method is to define the synchronization variable as a bit vector, with one bit corresponding to each iteration of the **doacross**. The bit vector is initialized to zero before the **doacross**. Each **post** statement simply requires setting the corresponding bit in the synchronization bit vector; a **wait** statement busy-waits until the appropriate bit is set. The generated code for the above case might look like:

```
        bit ASYNC(N)
        ASYNC(*) = '0'
        doacross I = 1, N
S₁:       A(I+1) = B(I) + C(I)
          ASYNC(I) = '1'
S₂:       D(I) = A(I+1) / 2
          if ( I-1 >= 1 ) wait for ( ASYNC(I-1) )
S₃:       C(I) = A(I)
        enddo
```

Notice the protection of the **wait** statement by an **if** to avoid an out-of-bounds reference. All the examples will have this protection, although with proper initialization the **if**s are not strictly necessary.

A second implementation uses only a single integer for synchronization. As would be expected, this reduces not only the storage required but also the flexibility and generality. The integer holds the last iteration number that has passed the **post** point. The **post** statement corresponds to setting this variable, while the **wait** statement busy-waits until the variable has reached or passed the required iteration. Naturally, **post** statements must now be sequenced in order, requiring more synchronization than would be necessary otherwise:

```
         integer ASYNC
         ASYNC = 0
         doacross I = 1, N
S₁:          A(I+1) = B(I) + C(I)
             if ( I-1 >= 1 ) wait until ( ASYNC >= I-1 )
             ASYNC = I
S₂:          D(I) = A(I+1) / 2
S₃:          C(I) = A(I)
         enddo
```

Notice that a **wait** is required before the **post** statement, essentially adding an empty critical section in the loop. In this particular example, this can replace the **wait** later in the loop; some cases may require two **wait**s: one to satisfy the dependence, and another to protect access to the synchronization variable. Lexically forward dependences are all satisfied by the empty critical section, so distance information is not important for these.

The third method is to use prescheduling and to have one integer per processor. Each processor will keep track of the last iteration to execute the **send**; since only one processor will update that word, no critical section around the update is necessary. A **wait** corresponds to a busy-wait for the word on the appropriate processor to reach that value:

```
         integer ASYNC (numberP)
         ASYNC(*) = 0
         doall p = 1, numberP
            do I = p, N, numberP
S₁:             A(I+1) = B(I) + C(I)
                ASYNC(p) = I
S₂:             D(I) = A(I+1) / 2
                if ( I-1 >= 1 ) then
                    wait until ( ASYNC(I-1 mod numberP) >= I-1 )
                endif
S₃:             C(I) = A(I)
            enddo
         enddo
```

The three implementations have very different cost tradeoffs. The bit vector method requires N bits to be allocated and initialized at the start of the loop. This may be fast for loops with small limits, but can be a significant time factor in some cases. Also, because of the need for an unknown number of bits (potentially many), the bit vector will probably have to be allocated in memory, not in processor registers. The single integer method has small initialization cost, but requires a critical section around the update. This is potentially a bottleneck or hot spot; however, the single word can probably be implemented as a special high speed hardware register. The word per processor method has low initialization cost, but requires prescheduling to fix the relationship between the iteration number and processor.

---

```
          event ASYNC
          doacross I = 1, N
              do J = 1, M
S₁:               A(I+1,J+1) = A(I+1,J) * B(I,J) + C(I,J)
                  post( ASYNC, I, J )
S₂:               D(I,J) = A(I+1,J+1) / 2
                  wait( ASYNC, I-1, J )
S₃:               C(I,J) = A(I,J+1)
              enddo
          enddo
```

**Figure 4.3.** Sample **doacross** loop which contains a serial loop.

---

## 4.6 Synchronization in Outer Concurrent Loops

Synchronization between iterations of an outer concurrent loop (which contains a serial loop) has more complications. An example is shown in Figure 4.3. Note that the **post** and **wait** must specify both the iteration of the concurrent loop and the serial loop. Here we survey four methods to implement this type of synchronization.

The first method is to use a bit array, similar to the bit vector approach used for a single loop. Here, the synchronization variable is an array (N×M) of bits; the **post** operation corresponds to setting the appropriate bit, and the **wait** waits until the proper bit is set. As in the previous section, the bit array approach suffers from the large amount of memory required and long initialization time.

The second method is to use a vector of words, with one word for each iteration of the inner loop. Each word tells what concurrent loop iteration has gotten this far in the serial loop. This works like the case of a single integer for a single parallel loop, in that a critical section is required around the update operation:

```
        array ASYNC(M)
        ASYNC(*) = 0
        doacross I = 1, N
            do J = 1, M
S₁:             A(I+1,J+1) = A(I+1,J) * B(I,J) + C(I,J)
                if ( I-1 >= 1 ) wait until ( ASYNC(J) >= I-1 )
                ASYNC(J) = I
S₂:             D(I,J) = A(I+1,J+1) / 2
S₃:             C(I,J) = A(I,J+1)
            enddo
        enddo
```

Again, the **wait** statement after $S_2$ is unnecessary due to the presence of the critical section. The **if** protecting the **wait** is not strictly necessary either,

Another method is to use an array of words, one for each iteration of the concurrent loop. This method requires no critical section around the update operation, since again only a single processor will update each word.

```
        array ASYNC(N)
        ASYNC(*) = 0
        doacross I = 1, N
            do J = 1, M
S₁:             A(I+1,J+1) = A(I+1,J) * B(I,J) + C(I,J)
                ASYNC(I) = J
S₂:             D(I,J) = A(I+1,J+1) / 2
                if ( I-1 >= 1 ) wait until ( ASYNC(I-1) >= J )
S₃:             C(I,J) = A(I,J+1)
            enddo
        enddo
```

Notice that in both this and the previous case, the **wait** operation needs the dependence distance in both the I and J loops.

If prescheduling is used, then the synchronization can be implemented with two words per processor:

```
          integer ASYNCI (numberP), ASYNCJ (numberP)
          ASYNCI (*) = 0
          ASYNCJ (*) = 0
          doall p = 1, numberP
             do I = p, N, numberP
                do J = 1, M
S₁:                   A(I+1,J+1) = A(I+1,J) * B(I,J) + C(I,J)
                      ASYNCI (p) = I
                      ASYNCJ (p) = J
S₂:                   D(I,J) = A(I+1,J+1) / 2
                      if( I-1 >= 1 ) then
                         wait until ( ASYNCI(I-1 mod numberP) > I-1
                         or (ASYNCI(I-1 mod numberP) = I-1
                         and ASYNCJ(I-1 mod numberP) > J ))
S₃:                   C(I,J) = A(I,J+1)
                enddo
             enddo
          enddo
```

The **wait** condition appears complex, but should be easy to implement in hardware.

The alternative to implementing multi-level synchronization primitives is to restrict synchronization to a single nest level. In that case, when a synchronization is required in an inner loop, either synchronization must be floated out of the inner loop (essentially creating a large critical section out of the inner loop), or the inner loop must be distributed. More experience in this area may prove fruitful in deciding on an efficient yet practical and useful paradigm.

# 5 Loop Fusion and Loop Scalarization

Loop fusion is the inverse of loop distribution; it is a well-known transformation in compiler optimization [AlCo72]. The traditional argument for doing loop fusion is to reduce the amount of loop overhead in a program; generally, this benefit is not enough to implement fusion in an optimizing compiler. For virtual memory machines, loop fusion can play a role in reducing the paging traffic in the memory hierarchy [AbuS78]. Yet, good tests for the validity of a loop fusion operation are not well known.

Here we will discover an important use for loop fusion for vector register machines. Since registers are the highest level of a memory hierarchy, it may be argued that loop fusion should reduce memory-register traffic; we shall see that it does. In fact, we shall see that fusion can reduce total memory requirements as well, in some cases.

We shall also find a new domain of application of loop fusion in vector languages. Applications of loop fusion in ordinary programs are rare, but a growing number of languages with vector and array syntax are appearing, and loop fusion can be used to optimize programs in these languages even for serial machines.

Finally, we shall derive a simple test for the validity of loop fusion. The test is based on the data dependence direction vectors of data dependence relations between the two loops.

## 5.1 Uses for Loop Fusion

Loop fusion will reduce the total amount of time spent on loop overhead in a program. A simple program is shown in Figure 5.1.

```
        do I = 1, N
S₁:        A(I) = B(I) + C(I)
        enddo
        do I = 1, N
S₂:        D(I) = A(I) * 2
        enddo
```

**Figure 5.1.** Example of candidate loops for loop fusion.

This program performs $2N$ increment-and-test operations. The same program with the loops fused is:

```
        do I = 1, N
S₁:        A(I) = B(I) + C(I)
S₂:        D(I) = A(I) * 2
        enddo
```

The transformed version will perform only N increment-and-test operations. However, this is a small savings, since loop control operations are often highly optimized in the computer hardware.

Abu-Sufah [AbuS78] discovered that loop fusion can help reduce paging traffic in a paged memory hierarchy system. In a sense, machine registers are another level in a memory hierarchy systems, so loop fusion should be useful in reducing traffic between registers and memory. Reducing register loads and stores is beneficial even for serial machines but it is even more interesting for machines with vector registers, since a vector register load is expensive.

In fact, loop fusion does reduce the amount of traffic necessary between registers and memory. If the program in Figure 5.1 were compiled for a serial machine with registers, each element of A computed in $S_1$ would be stored; then each element of A would be fetched in turn for $S_2$. After loop fusion, however, each element of A needed in $S_2$ would still be in a register, remaining there from the execution of $S_1$; thus, N register loads are saved. The same can be done for vector register loads and stores. An intelligent register assignment program will assign registers to reuse the values in a register whenever possible.

## 5.2. Loop Fusion in Vector Languages

In most ordinary programs the applicability of loop fusion is limited; few programmers write **do** loops that need loop fusion. There is a growing class of programs where loop fusion is very useful: programs written in a language with vector syntax. Programs are ofter easier to write in vector or array notation, easier to understand and maintain, and are more natural to the application; from the point of view of the programmer, a language with vector syntax may be "better" than a language without. Loop fusion is necessary to achieve the same performance in a vector language program as in a standard language program. Take for example the array assignments in Figure 5.2. These assignments perform the same computations as the program in Figure 5.1. If these assignments were compiled for a serial machine, they would be translated into a loop such as Figure 5.1. Without loop fusion, the resulting code would still have 2N increment-and-test operations. Similarly, if the array assignments were compiled for a vector register machine, without loop fusion the resulting code would have $2N/64$ increment-and-test operations (where 64 is the register length, or "strip-mine" length). Loop fusion would halve this number.

---

```
S₁:  A(1:N)  =  B(1:N)  +  C(1:N)
S₂:  D(1:N)  =  A(1:N)  *  2
```

**Figure 5.2.** Array assignments that are equivalent to the loops in Figure 5.1.

---

Another interesting result of loop fusion in vector syntax code is the possibility of reducing memory requirements. In scalar code, programmers often use scalar temporary variables; in vector or array code, it is likely that they will use vector or array temporary variables. A good optimizing compiler for scalar code will eliminate a "store" to a scalar temporary if all uses of the value are local, and it can be kept register-resident. When compiling vector code for serial machines or vector register machines, the values assigned to a vector temporary might possibly be kept register-resident, and the stores to the actual programmer temporary array might be eliminated. If there are no other uses of the programmer temporary array, the array itself may be deleted, saving memory space. In serial languages, deleting programmer temporary variables will free up only a small amount of memory, since each variable is only 1 (or a few) words. Vector temporaries can be quite large, however, and the space savings could be significant. Thus loop fusion can be applied to vector code to reduce loop overhead, memory-register traffic, and possibly total memory requirements.

If the array assignments above were compiled without loop fusion for a vector register machines, the resultant code would look like:

```
         do I = 1, N, 64
                 VL = MIN(64,N+1-I)
S1a:             vload v0, B(I), 1
S1b:             vload v1, C(I), 1
S1c:             vadd v2, v0, v1
S1d:             vstore v2, A(I), 1
         enddo
         do I = 1, N, 64
                 VL = MIN(64,N+1-I)
S2a:             vload v0, A(I), 1
S2b:             vmpy v1, s0, v0
S2c:             vstore v1, D(I), 1
         enddo
```

Here, as before, VL represents the vector length register, and v0, v1, ..., represent vector registers. Compiling the same program with loop fusion would give the code below:

```
         do I = 1, N, 64
                 VL = MIN(64,N+1-I)
S1a:             vload v0, B(I), 1
S1b:             vload v1, C(I), 1
S1c:             vadd v2, v0, v1
S1d:             vstore v2, A(I), 1
S2b:             vmpy v3, s0, v2
S2c:             vstore v3, D(I), 1
         enddo
```

Notice that fusing the loops allows the compiler to eliminate a register load, statement $S_{2a}$. In the original code, the array A is necessary to carry values from statement $S_1$ to $S_2$. After loop fusion, the array A is no longer needed for this purpose (although it may be necessary to carry values from $S_1$ to later statements). If no other statement uses the values stored into A by $S_1$, then the store (statement $S_{1d}$) can be eliminated also. If all uses of the array A are eliminated, then the storage for the array A can also be eliminated. A good dead code elimination algorithm would find the cases where useless stores could be eliminated; then any unused variables could also be deleted.

## 5.3 Test for Loop Fusion

To fuse two loops, the compiler must first test that the loop limits are identical. Occasionally the loop limits can be adjusted to make them identical, as in Figure 5.3. Sometimes the loop limits may differ by a small amount, as in Figure 5.4. In these cases, the loop limits may be made identical by unrolling one loop or by adding an **if** statement. Both choices have disadvantages; neither choice may be good unless the benefit from loop fusion is large.

Another test that must be passed for loop fusion to be legal is a data dependence test. For instance, the loops below are not fusible:

```
        do I = 1, N
S₁:       A(I) = B(I) + C(I)
        enddo
        do I = 1, N
S₂:       B(I+1) = D(I) * 2.
        enddo
```

---

```
        do I = 1, N
S₁:       A(I) = B(I) + C(I)
        enddo
        do I = 2, N+1
S₂:       D(I) = E(I) * 2
        enddo
```

    (a)

```
        do I = 1, N
S₁:       A(I) = B(I) + C(I)
        enddo
        do I = 1, N
S₂:       D(I+1) = E(I+1) * 2
        enddo
```

    (b)

**Figure 5.3.** Adjusting the loop limits to allow loop fusion. (a) Original loop limits are not fusible. (b) After adjusting the limits of the second loop allows fusion.

---

```
        do I = 1, N
S₁:        A(I) = B(I) + C(I)
        enddo
        do I = 2, N
S₂:        D(I) = E(I) * 2
        enddo

        (a)

        A(1) = B(1) + C(1)
        do I = 2, N
S₁:        A(I) = B(I) + C(I)
        enddo
        do I = 2, N
S₂:        D(I) = E(I) * 2
        enddo

        (b)

        do I = 1, N
S₁:        A(I) = B(I) + C(I)
        enddo
        do I = 1, N
S₂:        if (I > 1) D(I) = E(I) * 2
        enddo

        (c)
```

**Figure 5.4.** Adjusting the loop to change the loop limits. (a) Original loop limits are not fusible. (b) Unrolling the first loop makes the loops fusible. (c) Adding an **if** to the second loop also makes the loops fusible.

These loops have the data dependence relation $S_1 \; \overline{\delta} \; S_2$. Not all dependence relations disallow fusion (in Figure 5.1, $S_1 \; \delta \; S_2$, but the loops were still fusible), but this particular dependence relation changes is sensitive to fusion. If the loops are fused:

```
        do I = 1, N
S₁:        A(I) = B(I) + C(I)
S₂:        B(I+1) = D(I) * 2.
        enddo
```

the data dependence relation is changed to $S_2 \; \delta \; S_1$. Notice that fusion has changed the nature of the data dependence relation and has changed the semantics of the program. By using data dependence direction vectors augmented to add a direction for the adjacent loops (as introduced in section 2.3), the following test tells which data dependence relations prevent loop fusion.

**Lemma 5.1.**

For adjacent loops $L_1$ and $L_2$, if there is any statement $S_v$ in $L_1$ and $S_w$ in $L_2$ with $S_v \; \delta^*_{(>)} \; S_w$, then fusing the loops is illegal.

**Proof.**

The relation $S_v \; \delta^*_{(>)} \; S_w$ means that for some $i_0$ and $j_0$, $S_v[i_0] \; \delta^* \; S_w[j_0]$ and $i_0 > j_0$. Fusing the loops would mean that $S_w[j_0]$ would be executed before $S_v[i]$ for any $i > j_0$, thus violating the data dependence relation.

It is easily seen that the previous loop has a dependence relation $S_1 \; \bar{\delta}_{(>)} \; S_2$, and thus loop fusion is illegal.

Before two loops can be fused, several other conditions must be met. Obviously, the loops must be adjacent; if they are not, statement reordering may be able to make them adjacent. It is suggested that the compiler try the test in Lemma 5.1 before mangling the program via statement reordering.

Another condition is that neither loop may have a conditional branch which exits the loop. Fusing the loops would make the conditional exit leave both loops, which is not what the programmer had intended. Also, if both loops do input/output, then fusion will change the order of the I/O operations, making fusion illegal or inadvisable. If only one of the loops does I/O, then fusion will not affect the order of the operations and thus is okay.

## 5.4 Loop Scalarization

It was implied in Section 5.2 that a program written in a vector syntax could mindlessly be translated into serial code. Often this is true; for example, the array assignments in Figure 5.2 can be translated into the loops in Figure 5.1. In general, however, a mindless conversion of every vector statement into a serial loop is not legal. A four point difference operation is given in vector syntax below:

```
S₁: A(2:N-1,2:N-1)  =  (A(1:N-2,2:N-1)  +  A(2:N-1,1:N-2)  +
                        A(3:N,2:N-1)     +  A(2:N-1,3:N)) / 4
```

According to most (if not all) vector language semantics, this statement should perform all the operations specified on the right hand side before performing any stores; all the operations are done with "old" values of the array A. A mindless conversion into serial code, is illegal in this case since the serial loop uses "new" values of the array A in the right hand side computation:

```
     do I = 2, N-1
        do J = 2, N-1
S₁:        A(I,J)  =  (A(I-1,J)  +  A(I,J-1)  +
                       A(I+1,J)  +  A(I,J+1)) / 4
        enddo
     enddo
```

A legal translation is given below; all the operations are performed using "old" values of A,

94

and saved in a compiler temporary array. The second loop stores the computed values back into A:

```
        do I = 2, N-1
           do J = 2, N-1
  S₁ₐ:        T(I,J) = (A(I-1,J) + A(I,J-1) +
                         A(I+1,J) + A(I,J+1)) / 4
           enddo
        enddo
        do I = 2, N-1
           do J = 2, N-1
  S₁ᵦ:        A(I,J) = T(I,J)
           enddo
        enddo
```

Translating vector code into two consecutive serial loops (as above) always works. The first loop performs the computations and the second loop performs the stores. Of course the compiler must generate a compiler temporary array, perhaps an undesirable requirement. The compiler temporary is obviously not necessary all the time, and a simple test will indicate which cases can be more simply translated. If these two loops can be fused, then statement substitution will eliminate the redundant assignment and the need for the compiler temporary array. Note that the only kind of dependence that can prevent this fusion is a data anti-dependence (since there is no output dependence between the two loops, and the flow dependence has an equal direction). If there is an anti-dependence with a (>) direction, then loop fusion is illegal. Testing for legal loop fusion of the adjacent serial loops is equivalent to testing for an anti-dependence from the right hand side of the array assignment to the left hand side.

*Example.* The array assignment below:

$$S_1: \quad A(1:N) = A(2:N+1) + B(1:N)$$

has the data dependence relation $S_1 \ \overline{\delta}_{(<)} \ S_1$. Even though the left hand side variable is used on the right hand side, it can be trivially scalarized:

```
        do I = 1, N
  S₁:      A(I) = A(I+1) + B(I)
        enddo
```

However, the following array assignment:

$$S_1: \quad A(2:N+1) = A(1:N) + B(1:N)$$

has the data dependence relation $S_1 \ \overline{\delta}_{(>)} \ S_1$, which prevents simple scalarization. However, by reversing the index set, i.e., running the loop backwards, the (>) can be changed to a (<), and scalarization is possible.

```
          do I = N, 1, -1
S₁:         A(I+1) = A(I) + B(I)
          enddo
```

If we treat array assignments as being written with **forall** statements, then the four-point difference equation above would be:

```
          forall I = 2, N-1
            forall J = 2, N-1
S₁:           A(I,J) = (A(I-1,J) + A(I,J-1) +
                         A(I+1,J) + A(I,J+1)) / 4
            endforall
          endforall
```

The assignment has $S_1 \, \overline{\delta}_{(>,=)} \, S_1$ and $S_1 \, \overline{\delta}_{(=,>)} \, S_1$, which prevent simple scalarization of either of the vector **forall**s. Note that loop reversal won't work either, since the assignment also has the relations $S_1 \, \overline{\delta}_{(<,=)} \, S_1$ and $S_1 \, \overline{\delta}_{(=,<)} \, S_1$, which would be changed by loop reversal to $(>)$ directions, again preventing simple scalarization.

Correctly and efficiently translating vector code to serial code is important in compilers for serial machines. It is also necessary in compilers for vector machines, since the semantics of the machine instructions may not match the semantics of the language, and to scalarize vector statements with more than one degree of parallelism.

# 6 Loop Interchanging

Loop interchanging, the process of switching inner and outer loops, is the most powerful of the transformations presented here. It has a profound effect on the execution order of a loop and can therefore have a large effect on the performance of a loop on various machines. Recently, commercial compilers and translators have become available that perform loop interchanging.

There are several reasons to interchange loops. For machines with vector instructions, loops can be interchanged to find vector operations. That is, if the inner loop cannot be vectorized, the loops may be interchanged to bring a loop that can be vectorized to the innermost position.

Some machines perform better when all array references are stride-1 (that is, the vector operands are stored in consecutive memory locations). The vector operations of the Cyber 205 require the arrays to be contiguous. In other machines which allow non-unit strides, performance is degraded for certain strides; ensuring unit stride guarantees the best performance of the memory. Loop interchanging can be used to increase the number of stride-1 array accesses in a loop.

Yet another use for loop interchanging is to increase the number of scalar operands in the inner loop. This is simply a special case of loop interchanging to increase locality of memory references in the loop, to improve the performance of memory hierarchies. Vector registers can be treated as a level in the memory hierarchy, and we show how to reduce vector register loads and stores using this technique. In the same fashion paging traffic in a paged virtual memory system can be reduced.

For multiprocessor machines, parallel outer loops are preferred. Loop interchanging may be able to switch parallel loops to the outer position when the original outer loop is not parallel.

For all machines, large loop limits give better performance. Vector machines work better with long vectors than with short vectors. Multiprocessors likewise perform better when many parallel operations are possible. Loop interchanging can be used to switch loops to get the longest loop limits in the best position for the target machine.

Of paramount importance when interchanging loops is preserving correct results in the program. The compiler can use a simple test for loop interchanging based on the data dependence direction vector. We will also show how to interchange triangular loops, where the limits of the inner loop depend on the outer loop index, as well as other advanced loop interchanging techniques. Finally, we can show that loop interchanging is result-preserving; unlike other program transformations such as fast recurrence solvers, no roundoff error changes are introduced by interchanging loops. In fact, the same computations are performed on the same data after loops are interchanged as before; just the order of computing is different.

Many goals can be satisfied by loop interchanging; the goals are different depending on the particular target machine. We show how to choose goals for a given machine.

## 6.1 Loop Interchanging Data Dependence Test

The simplest example of loop interchanging is interchanging two nested loops, such as the loops below:

```
do I = 1, N
    do J = 1, M
        do K = 1, P
            A(I,J) = A(I,J) + B(I,K)*C(K,J)
        enddo
    enddo
enddo
```

The inner loop above is a dot product. If this loop were compiled for a vector oriented machine that had a fast dot product or vector sum instruction, the inner loop could be translated directly into vector instructions. If these instructions were missing or were slow, then loop interchanging could transform the loop into:

```
do J = 1, M
    do K = 1, P
        do I = 1, N
            A(I,J) = A(I,J) + B(I,K)*C(K,J)
        enddo
    enddo
enddo
```

The new inner loop can be compiled as a vector multiply followed by a vector add. No reduction operation is necessary, and in addition, assuming Fortran column-major storage order, all array accesses are stride-1. For some machines, the interchanged loop would execute faster than the original loop.

Obviously, not all loop interchanges are legal. For instance, the loops below may not be interchanged:

```
do I = 2, N
    do J = 1, N-1
        A(I,J) = A(I-1,J+1) + B(I,J)
    enddo
enddo
```

The original loop uses newly computed values of the array A on the right hand side; if the loops are interchanged, the transformed loop will use only old values of A on the right hand side. The transformed loop will compute different results and the transformation is thus illegal.

**Lemma 6.1.**

The requirements for simple loop interchanging can be stated as:

1) the loops $L'$ and $L''$ must be tightly nested ($L'$ surrounds $L''$, but contains no other executable statements),
2) the loop limits of $L''$ are invariant in $L'$,
3) there are no statements $S_v$ and $S_w$ (not necessarily distinct) in $L''$ with a dependence relation $S_v \, \delta^*_{(<,>)} \, S_w$.

**Proof.**

Suppose $S_v \, \delta^*_{(<,>)} \, S_w$. Then there are values $i_1$, $i_2$ and $j_1$, $j_2$ where

$$i_1 < j_1, i_2 > j_2 \text{ and } S_v[i_1, i_2] \, \delta^* \, S_w[j_1, j_2]$$

If the loops are interchanged, then $S_w[j_1, j_2]$ will be executed before $S_v[i_1, i_2]$ since $j_2 < i_2$, thus violating the data dependence relation. Suppose there are no dependence relations with $(<,>)$ direction vectors. The only possible dependence direction vectors between statements in the loop are

$$(<,<) \qquad (<,=) \qquad (=,<) \qquad (=,=)$$

Now, suppose there is a dependence relation $S_v \, \delta^*_{(<,<)} \, S_w$. Then there are values $i_1$, $i_2$ and $j_1$, $j_2$ where

$$i_1 < j_1, i_2 < j_2 \text{ and } S_v[i_1, i_2] \, \delta^* \, S_w[j_1, j_2]$$

If the loops are interchanged, then $S_v[i_1, i_2]$ will still be executed before $S_w[j_1, j_2]$, thus satisfying the data dependence relations. A similar argument holds for the directions $(<,=)$, $(=,<)$ and $(=,=)$. As in vectorization, any dependence relations with a forward direction in an outer loop (containing $L'$) can be ignored.

Allen and Kennedy [Kenn80, AlKe84, AlKe87] give another data dependence test for loop interchanging. Their test is a modification of Banerjee's data dependence test [Bane76] that is equivalent to a test for a $(=,=...,=,<,>)$ data dependence direction vector, as pointed out in their papers.

If there are input or output statements, then interchanging the loops will change the order in which the I/O occurs. This may be allowable for direct access I/O or for print output, but in general it is not allowable for the compiler to change the order of I/O operations of a program. This can generally be modeled by adding IO dependence arcs to the dependence graph.

The simple rules above require invariant inner loop limits. This restriction can sometimes be relaxed, as we will see in the next section, but the general case may be intractable, as when the limits of the inner loop are array references. Also, the rules above require tightly nested loops; this also can be relaxed, or else loop distribution can be used to distribute a non-tightly nested outer loop around an inner loop to promote interchanging.

## 6.2 Goals for Loops Interchanging

Several goals can be met by the compiler via loop interchanging. This fact makes loop interchanging the most powerful high-level optimization which a compiler can perform. The particular goals are very machine specific, but general concepts can also be derived. We will first discuss general goals for which a compiler might interchange loops, and then identify which goals apply to different machines.

**Vectorizable Inner Loops.** Vectorizable inner loops are necessary to utilize the vector instruction set of a vector computer. The compiler may come across an inner loop which is not vectorizable, or which needs an instruction not in the instruction set of the target machine. For instance, the inner loop below:

```
do I = 1, N
    do J = 1, N
        A(I,J+1) = A(I,J)*B(I,J) + C(I,J)
    enddo
enddo
```

is a first order linear recurrence; most vector computers have no corresponding instruction, so the loop would be executed serially, or with some fast recurrence algorithm. By interchanging the loops:

```
do J = 1, N
    do I = 1, N
        A(I,J+1) = A(I,J)*B(I,J) + C(I,J)
    enddo
enddo
```

the inner loop is vectorizable, and can be computed with a vector multiply followed by a vector add.

**Parallel Outer Loops.** When compiling for a multiprocessor, parallel loops are desired. These parallel loops need not be the outer loops for parallel execution on a multiprocessor, but less synchronization time is required if they are. When the parallel loop is an inner loop, as below:

```
do I = 1, N
    doall J = 1, N
        A(I+1,J) = A(I,J)*B(I,J) + C(I,J)
    enddo
enddo
```

the machine will execute the outer loop serially, then fork into parallel processes to execute the inner loop, synchronize at the end of the inner parallel loop, then continue with the serial code;

100

this is a total of N forks and joins. With the loops interchanged:

```
doall J = 1, N
    do I = 1, N
        A(I+1,J) = A(I,J)*B(I,J) + C(I,J)
    enddo
enddo
```

the machine will fork into parallel processes to execute the outer loop, and each process will execute the inner loop serially, independently of other processes; a single fork and join is necessary.

**Stride-1 Array References.** Many computers work better when arrays are accessed in a stride-1 manner. A stride-1 array reference is a reference which will access contiguous elements of the array on consecutive iterations of a loop. The vector instructions of some computers work only on contiguous arrays (such as the ETA 10); for other machines the memory slows down for certain strides, but unit stride ensures full memory speed (such as the Crays, which slows down for strides that are multiples of the number of memory banks).

If we assume column-major storage order (as in Fortran), then the inner loop below has four non-stride-1 array references; for each array, the stride for the J-dimension is 20:

```
real A(20,30), B(20,30), C(20,30)

do I = 1, N
    do J = 1, M
        A(I,J) = B(I,J) + A(I,J)*C(I,J)
    enddo
enddo
```

There are three ways to change these references into stride-1 references. The first is to transpose each array at compile-time, i.e., to store the array in row-major order:

```
real A(30,20), B(30,20), C(30,20)

do I = 1, N
    do J = 1, M
        A(J,I) = B(J,I) + A(J,I)*C(J,I)
    enddo
enddo
```

This is possible only if all references to the array can be transposed, and the array is local to the program unit being compiled (not passed to external routines which expect the array in canonical order, and not in a Fortran COMMON block) or the array can be transposed in all external routines also. The CDC Fortran 200 compiler for the Cyber 205 provides a directive, the ROWWISE statement, by which the programmer tells the compiler to transpose the array at compile time.

The second way to change non-stride-1 array references into stride-1 array references is to transpose the array at run time. This requires extra operations, but the machine may have a fast transpose instruction sequence:

```
real A(20,30), B(20,30), C(20,30)
real AT(30,20), BT(30,20), CT(30,20)

AT(1:M,1:N) = TRANSPOSE(A(1:N,1:M))
BT(1:M,1:N) = TRANSPOSE(B(1:N,1:M))
CT(1:M,1:N) = TRANSPOSE(C(1:N,1:M))
do I = 1, N
    do J = 1, M
        AT(I,J) = BT(I,J) + AT(I,J)*CT(I,J)
    enddo
enddo
A(1:N,1:M) = TRANSPOSE(AT(1:M,1:N))
```

This may be cost-effective only when the number of uses of each variable that must be transposed is large, amortizing the cost of the transpose operation.

The third way to change non-stride-1 array references into stride-1 array references is to interchange the loops so that the stride-1 index becomes the inner loop:

```
real A(20,30), B(20,30), C(20,30)

do J = 1, M
    do I = 1, N
        A(I,J) = B(I,J) + A(I,J)*C(I,J)
    enddo
enddo
```

Interchanging loops is a good way to do this, since the array storage sequence is not modified (as by compile time transposing) and no extra operations are required (as by run-time transposing); of course, the loops must be interchangeable. The biggest disadvantage is that interchanging the loops will affect all array references, not just those that were non-stride-1; in particular, interchanging can also (obviously) change stride-1 array references into non-stride-1 array references. For this reason, the best solution to the non-stride-1 array reference problem is a combination of these three techniques.

**Invariant Operands.** An invariant operand in a loop can be fetched from memory once at the beginning of the loop and used throughout the execution of the loop. Loop interchanging can be used to increase the number of invariant operands in a loop. For example, the inner loop below has two array input operands, A and B:

102

```
do J = 1, N
    do I = 1, N
        A(I,J) = C(I,J)*B(J)
    enddo
enddo
```

By interchanging the loops, the B operand becomes invariant in the inner loop and can be kept in a register for the duration of that loop:

```
do I = 1, N
    do J = 1, N
        A(I,J) = C(I,J)*B(J)
    enddo
enddo
```

Occasionally loop interchanging can uncover loop invariant operations, which can be floated out by code motion.

**Longer Loop Limits.** All supercomputers work with better efficiency when the longest loops (loops with the largest number of iterations) are being done in parallel. For vector machines, this means that long loops should be inner loops for which vector code is generated. For multiprocessors with a large number of processors, the long loops should be outer loops (if possible) and be done in parallel. For multiprocessors with a small number of processor, the short loops should be outer loops, done in parallel, and the long loops should be inner loops, done serially in each processor. Loop interchanging can be used to move the longest loop to the innermost or outermost position.

## 6.3 Matching Goals for Loop Interchanging to Machines

As was seen in the previous section, loop interchanging can serve many purposes; some of the goals mentioned may be conflicting. For instance, interchanging loops to make array references stride-1 may bring a non-vectorizable loop to the innermost position. In this section we study the possible criteria and machine architectures, to match the criteria to the machines.

**Memory-to-Memory Pipelined Machines.** The memory-to-memory pipelined machine is exemplified by the ETA 10; it has fast vector operations for consecutive operands, a rather long vector startup time, and the capability for linked triad operations (when one operand is a scalar). The most important criterion for this machine is vectorizable inner loops. Since the vector instructions work with consecutive vectors, stride-1 array references are also important. The long vector startup time means that long vectors (long inner loops) are also desired. These requirements must be balanced; choosing between short vectors with stride-1 array references and long vectors without stride-1 references must be done carefully, perhaps with empirical knowledge. Also, increasing the number of invariant operands increases the likelihood of finding a linked triad operation.

**Vector Register Pipelined Machines.** The vector register pipelined machine is exemplified by the Cray computers; it has fast vector instructions that work on operands in its vector registers, and a short vector startup time. Again, the most important criterion is a vectorizable inner loop. Stride-1 array references are not necessary, but do not hurt. The short vector startup time means that long vectors are not so important, but the longer the vector, the better the efficiency (in general). Loop invariant operands are beneficial since they can be kept in a scalar register, instead of a scarce vector register.

An interesting twist to the concept of interchanging loops to increase invariant operands shows up when compiling for vector register machines. One advantage to finding a loop invariant scalar is that the scalar can be loaded into a register once outside the loop, instead of being loaded many times inside the loop. With a vector register machine, a loop invariant vector can be loaded into a vector register outside the loop. For example, in a matrix multiply:

```
        do I = 1, N
          do J = 1, M
            do K = 1, P
S₁:            A(I,J) = A(I,J) + B(I,K)*C(K,J)
            enddo
          enddo
        enddo
```

For a Cray-like machine, the loops might be interchanged (to get a vector operation and stride-1 array references), the inner loop would be strip mined as required to the register length, and vector code would be generated:

```
        do J = 1, M
          do K = 1, P
            load    s0, C[K,J]
            do I = 1, N, 64
S₁ₐ:          vload   v0, A[I,J], 1
S₁ᵦ:          vload   v1, B[I,J], 1
S₁ᵪ:          vmpy    v1, s0, v2
S₁d:          vadd    v0, v2, v0
S₁ₑ:          vstore  v0, A[I,J], 1
            enddo
          enddo
        enddo
```

The inner loop contains five vector instructions; instructions $S_{1b}$, $S_{1c}$, and $S_{1d}$ can be chained. The ratio of memory to arithmetic instructions on this loop is 3 to 2, meaning that the code is heavily memory bandwidth limited. By interchanging loops differently so that the strip mine loop is not the innermost serial loop, the vector register load and store of A becomes invariant in the **do** K loop:

```
        do J = 1, M
            do I = 1, N, 64
S1a:            vload v0, A[I,J], 1
                do K = 1, P
                    load    s0, C[K,J]
S1b:                vload   v1, B[I,J], 1
S1c:                vmpy    v1, s0, v2
S1d:                vadd    v0, v2, v0
                enddo
S1e:            vstore v0, A[I,J], 1
            enddo
        enddo
```

Now the inner loop contains only three vector instructions, and only one vector memory reference.

**Multiprocessors.** The multiprocessor is exemplified by the Sequent computers; they can execute parallel loops and again have a non-trivial loop startup time. Parallel outer loops are the first criterion (as opposed to vectorizable inner loops). If a large number of processors is available, then long parallel loops are desired; this can be satisfied by finding long individual loops, or by finding nested parallel loops and doing the whole iteration space in parallel. If a small number of processors is available, then shorter parallel loops are desired; each processor should be assigned a large block of code to be executed concurrently with other processors. Putting the long loops in the inner position and executing them serially will satisfy this desire. Stride-1 array references might hurt by causing cache conflicts between the processors (stride-1 in the parallel loop index, not necessarily the inner loop index).

**Virtual Memory Machines.** In a paged virtual memory machine environment, loop interchanging can also be helpful. Any array reference might cause a page fault; a page fault is similar to an implicit vector register load, so the criteria for interchanging loops for virtual memory machines should be similar to criteria for reducing traffic between vector registers and memory. If the machine has no vector instructions then finding vectorizable loops is of no value. However, increasing the number of stride-1 array references will also increase the locality of array references which should reduce page faults. Also, increasing the number of invariant operands is useful; this includes both the number of scalar operands and the number of invariant "page load" operations (conceptually similar to a "vector register load" operation). Loops may be strip mined to the page size as for a vector register machine. For example, the original program below would access a new page in each iteration of the **do** J loop for the array A (assuming each column of the array A takes at least one page):

```
do I = 1, N
    do J = 1, M
        A(I,J) = 4 * E(I)
    enddo
enddo
```

If only two pages were allocated, then N*M page faults would occur for the array A, and $\frac{N}{z}$ page faults for the array E (where $z$ is the page size). By interchanging the loops:

```
do J = 1, M
    do I = 1, N
        A(I,J) = 4 * E(I)
    enddo
enddo
```

only $\frac{N*M}{z}$ page faults are required for the array A, while the number required for the array E has not changed.

Exactly the same technique will improve the hit ratio for a hardware managed cache memory. Notice that this technique has nothing to do with parallelism discovery, and can be applied to scalar computers also; one (uncontrolled) experiment on a VAX showed a dramatic performance improvement due entirely to reduced page faults.

In fact, vectorization often reduces locality of reference. When a loop is vectorized, a statement will refer to a whole vector before that vector can be reused. If the vector length is larger than the cache or physical memory size, then thrashing can occur. Vectorization does, in general, increase predictability of memory references, meaning that smart hardware may be able to preload pages or cache lines for the vector operations. The non-locality of vectorization can be attacked by strip mining the loop.

Abu-Sufah [AbuS78, AbKL81] discussed the square-block array storage scheme for paged virtual memory machines. In this machine, a page is a square submatrix of an array instead of a column. The advantage of this storage scheme is that loops which access some array by rows and some arrays by columns can be efficiently transformed to reduce page faults dramatically over column-major or row-major storage schemes. Loop interchanging plays a large role in transforming programs to reduce page faults for square-block array storage virtual memory machines.

## 6.4 Triangular Loop Interchanging

When the limits of the inner loop depend on the outer loop index, the loop can traverse a triangular iteration space, as shown in Figure 6.1. There are eight triangular shapes possible (upper/lower, left/right, with/without diagonal).

lower left triangle:
```
do I = 1, N
    do J = 1, I [1, I-1]
```

upper right triangle:
```
do I = 1, N
    do J = I, N [I+1, N]
```

upper left triangle:
```
do I = 1, N
    do J = 1, N-I+1 [1,N-I]
```

lower right triangle:
```
do I = 1, N
    do J = N-I+1, N [N-I, N]
```

**Figure 6.1.** Examples of triangular loops; loop limits for the cases without the diagonal are in square brackets.

interchanged lower left triangle: 
```
do J = 1, N
    do I = J, N [J+1, N]
```

interchanged upper right triangle: 
```
do J = 1, N
    do I = 1, J [1, J-1]
```

interchanged upper left triangle: 
```
do J = 1, N
    do I = 1, N-J+1 [1,N-J]
```

interchanged lower right triangle: 
```
do J = 1, N
    do I = N-J+1, N [N-J, N]
```

**Figure 6.2.** Examples of triangular loops from Figure 6.1 after proper interchanging; loop limits for the cases without the diagonal are in square brackets.

The data dependence test for interchanging triangular loops is the same as for any other loop. However, the compiler must properly modify the loop limits so that the loop will traverse the same iteration space, albeit in a different order. This is similar to interchanging the indices of a double summation. Figure 6.2 shows each example from Figure 6.1 with the loop interchanged and the loop limits properly modified. Note that loop interchanging essentially transposes the iteration space through the major diagonal, changing a lower left triangular loop into an upper right triangular loop, and so on; upper left and lower right triangles are symmetric about this diagonal.

**Trapezoidal Iteration Spaces.** Triangular loop limits can produce non-triangular iteration space shapes if the invariant inner loop limit is not identical to the corresponding outer loop limit:

```
do I = 1, N
    do J = I, M
```

To interchange the loops, the J loop limits must cover the entire possible range of J:

```
do J = 1, M
    do I = 1, J
```

The limits for the I shown above are almost correct, but would traverse too large an iteration space. Suppose M > N; then these loop limits would traverse up to iteration [I=M, J=M], where the original loop never got farther than I=N. In effect, these loop limits define a larger iteration space than desired:

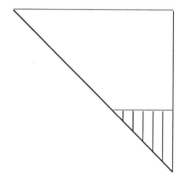

By adjusting the limits to cut off the undesired lower point, we get the correct result:

```
do J = 1, M
    do I = 1, MIN(N,J)
```

As with triangular loops, there are four types of trapezoidal loop, as shown in Figure 6.3. They can be interchanged by changing the loop limits as shown in Figure 6.4. A little study will show that triangular loop interchanging is really a special case of trapezoidal loop interchanging, with the MIN and MAX calls optimized out.

There is no reason why both the upper and lower limits of the inner loop could not contain the outer loop index:

```
do I = 1, N
    do J = I, N+I
```

Loop interchanging can be accomplished by treating the upper and lower limits individually:

```
do J = 1, N+N
    do I = MAX(1,J-N), MIN(J,N)
```

lower left trapezoid:
```
do I = LBI, UBI
    do J = LBJ, UBJ+I
```

upper right trapezoid:
```
do I = LBI, UBI
    do J = LBJ+I, UBJ
```

upper left trapezoid:
```
do I = LBI, UBI
    do J = LBJ, UBJ-I
```

lower right trapezoid:
```
do I = LBI, UBI
    do J = LBJ-I, UBJ
```

**Figure 6.3.** Examples of trapezoidal iteration loops.

interchanged lower left trapezoid:
```
do J = LBJ, UBJ+UBI
    do I = MAX(J-UBJ,LBI), UBI
```

interchanged upper right trapezoid:
```
do J = LBJ+LBI, UBJ
    do I = LBI, MIN(J-LBJ,UBJ)
```

interchanged upper left trapezoid:
```
do J = LBJ, UBJ-LBI
    do I = LBI, MIN(UBJ-J,UBI)
```

interchanged lower right trapezoid:
```
do J = LBJ-UBI, UBJ
    do I = MAX(LBJ-J,LBI), UBJ
```

**Figure 6.4.** Examples of trapezoidal loops from Figure 6.3 after interchanging.

Even pathological cases, such as:
```
do I = 1, N
    do J = I, M-I
```
can be interchanged by taking the limits one at a time:
```
do J = 1, M-1
    do I = 1, MIN(J,M-J,N)
```

**Loop Normalization.** Another aspect of triangular loops that is interesting is how they are affected by *loop normalization*. This is a simple transformation [KKLW80, BCKT79, AlKe87] to "normalize" the **do** loop limits so that other compiler functions, such as data dependence calculation, are simplified. Loop normalization changes the limits of each loop so that the loop begins at 1 (or 0) and has an increment of 1; the upper limit is changed accordingly. For example the loop below:

```
do I = 2, N, 3
    A(I) = B(I+1)
enddo
```

would be modified by normalization to become:

```
do I = 1, (N-1)/3
    A(I*3-1) = B(I*3)
enddo
```

Each reference to the loop index variable is changed into a simple expression.

Usually loop normalization is a harmless transformation; but consider how the loops below would be normalized:

```
do I = 1, N
    do J = I, N
S₁          A(I,J) = A(I-1,J)
    enddo
enddo
```

The only dependence relation in this loop is $S_1 \; \delta_{(<,=)} \; S_1$. The outer loop is already in normal form, but the inner loop would need to be modified:

```
do I = 1, N
    do J = 1, N-I+1
S₁          A(I,J+I-1) = A(I-1,J+I-1)
    enddo
enddo
```

The data dependence relation is $S_1 \; \delta_{(<,>)} \; S_1$ (since $S_1 [1, 3] \; \delta \; S_1 [2, 2]$). Loop normalization, in changing the shape of the iteration space, has changed the direction of the data dependence relations. In this example, the original loops could be interchanged; the normalized loops can not (due to the $(<,>)$ data dependence direction vector). Also, the subscript expressions now involve more than one loop index variable; this means that the data dependence tests will be more expensive (time consuming). Thus loop normalization, even though it is a trivial transformation, should be done carefully and selectively to achieve best results.

As shown above, loop normalization will change an upper or lower right triangular loop into an upper or lower left triangular loop; We have seen that this can be detrimental in certain circumstances. In fact, this may lead us to modify the loop normalization transformation to

110

change upper and lower left triangular loops of into upper and lower right forms, in the hopes of changing a (<,>) data dependence direction into a (<,=) direction, which will then allow the loops to be interchanged. For triangular loops this is probably not a bad idea (except that array subscripts may get more complex). Another question is whether changing the shape of the iteration space can be applied in other ways; this is taken up again Chapter 8.

## 6.5 Imperfectly Nested Loops

Often a compiler will come across imperfectly nested loops where loop interchanging is desired. At least two ways of handling this have been developed: loop distribution, and the Non-Basic-to-Basic-Loop transformation of Abu-Sufah [AbuS78].

Loop distribution can be used to distribute the outer loop around the inner loop, resulting in tightly nested loops which can be interchanged in the normal manner. The data dependence test for loop distribution is given in Chapter 3.

*Example.* An imperfectly nested loop is shown below:

```
L₁:  do I = 1, N
S₁:       T(I) = T(I) + 1
L₂:       do J = 2, M
S₂:            A(I,J) = B(I,J) + A(I,J-1)*T(I)
          enddo
     enddo
```

The inner loop $L_2$ cannot be vectorized. The loops cannot be immediately interchanged, but $L_1$ can be distributed:

```
L₁ₐ: do I = 1, N
S₁:       T(I) = T(I) + 1
     enddo
L₁ᵦ: do I = 1, N
L₂:       do J = 2, M
S₂:            A(I,J) = B(I,J) + A(I,J-1)*T(I)
          enddo
     enddo
```

Now loops $L_{1b}$ and $L_2$ can be interchanged:

```
L1a : do I = 1, N
S1 :      T(I) = T(I) + 1
          enddo
L2 : do J = 2, M
L1b :      do I = 1, N
S2 :            A(I,J) = B(I,J) + A(I,J-1)*T(I)
           enddo
      enddo
```

Notice that the inner loop is now vectorizable.

The data dependence test for loop distribution can be done at the same time as the data dependence test for loop interchanging, by looking at the data dependence relations between statements in the outer loop. Statement reordering may be necessary to allow loop distribution around the inner loop.

The Non-Basic-to-Basic-Loop transformation is not so promising. This was designed to be used when loop distribution is illegal. A "basic loop" is a tightly nested loop. This transformation creates a tightly nested loop by bringing all the statements into the inner loop, adding **if** statements as necessary for correct execution.

*Example.* The loop below shows how the previous example would be transformed into a basic loop by this transformation. After transforming a loop into a basic loop, the normal loop interchanging tests can continue:

```
L1 : do I = 1, N
L2 :      do J = 2, M
S1 :            if ( J=2 ) T(I) = T(I) + 1
S2 :            A(I,J) = B(I,J) + A(I,J-1)*T(I)
           enddo
       enddo
```

The problem is that it generally does not help. If loop distribution is illegal, then there is a data dependence relation with a forward direction either from a statement inside the inner loop to a statement above the inner loop (as in Figure 6.5) or from a statement below the inner loop to a statement in the inner loop (as in Figure 6.6). In either case, unless there is a cycle of dependence, statement reordering can be used to allow loop distribution, so we will assume a cycle of dependence.

```
        do I = 1, N
S₁:         T(I) = F(I)*A(I-1,5)
        do J = 1, M
S₂:            A(I,J) = T(I) + B(I,J)
        enddo
    enddo
```

**Figure 6.5.** Non-basic loop with the dependence cycle due to the relations $S_1 \, \delta_{(=)} \, S_2$ and $S_2 \, \delta_{(<)} \, S_1$.

```
        do I = 1, N
        do J = 1, M
S₁:            A(I,J) = T(I) + B(I,J)
        enddo
S₂:        T(I) = A(I,5)*F(I)
    enddo
```

**Figure 6.6.** Non-basic loop with a dependence cycle due to the relations $S_1 \, \delta_{(=)} \, S_2$ and $S_2 \, \delta_{(<)} \, S_1$.

Suppose the loop in Figure 6.5 is changed to a basic loop, as below:

```
        do I = 1, N
        do J = 1, M
S₁:            if( J=1 ) T(I) = F(I)*A(I-1,5)
S₂:            A(I,J) = T(I) + B(I,J)
        enddo
    enddo
```

The dependence relations of the transformed loop are $S_1 \, \delta_{(=,\,\leq)} \, S_2$ and $S_2 \, \delta_{(<,\,*)} \, S_1$; the relation from $S_2$ to $S_1$ disallows any loop interchanging, due to the potential $(<, >)$ direction vector. If the loop in Figure 6.6 were translated to a basic loop, again loop interchanging would be illegal.

There is one case where the Non-Basic-to-Basic Loop transformation will still allow loop interchanging. When the dependence relation from the inner loop is a dependence from the first iteration of the inner loop, then after transforming the loop to a basic loop, loop interchanging is still legal. For example, in the loop below:

```
        do I = 1, N
S₁:        T(I) = F(I)*A(I-1,1)
           do J = 1, M
S₂:            A(I,J) = T(I) + B(I,J)
           enddo
        enddo
```

the dependence relations $S_1 \, \delta_{(=)} \, S_2$ and $S_2 \, \delta_{(<)} \, S_1$ still exist, as in Figure 6.5. However, the relation $S_2 \, \delta_{(<)} \, S_1$ applies only for $S_2[I,1] \, \delta \, S_1[I+1]$. After transforming this to a basic loop:

```
        do I = 1, N
           do J = 1, M
S₁:            if( J=1 ) T(I) = F(I)*A(I-1,1)
S₂:            A(I,J) = T(I) + B(I,J)
           enddo
        enddo
```

the lexically backward arc changes to $S_2 \, \delta_{(<,\le)} \, S_1$, so loop interchanging is still legal.

However, in this same case, another method will allow loop distribution to be applied. The inner loop can be "unrolled" one iteration:

```
        do I = 1, N
S₁:        T(I) = F(I)*A(I-1,1)
S₂ₐ:       A(I,1) = T(I) + B(I,1)
           do J = 2, M
S₂:            A(I,J) = T(I) + B(I,J)
           enddo
        enddo
```

This introduces no **if** statement overhead and allows loop fission and loop interchanging in exactly those cases where the Non-Basic-to-Basic Loop transformation allows loop interchanging. A similar case occurs when the cycle of dependence involves only the last iteration of the inner loop.

## 6.6 Interchanging Imperfectly Nested Loops Directly

Rather than converting imperfectly nested loops to perfectly nested loops to allow interchanging, we can directly interchange imperfectly nested loops. For instance, the loop:

```
        do I = 1, N
S₁:        ... A(I) ...
        do J = 1, N
S₂:            ... B(I,J) ...
        enddo
S₃:        ... C(I) ...
        enddo
```

$S_2$ represents the body of the J loop, and $S_1$ and $S_3$ represent the parts of body of the I loop lexically above and below the J loop. The iteration space of this loop has separate parts for $S_1$, $S_2$ and $S_3$:

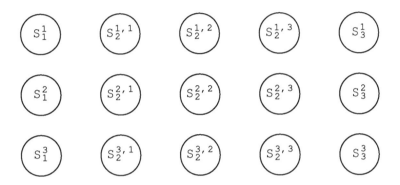

Interchanging the two loops directly results in:

```
        do J = 1, N
S₁:        ... A(J) ...
        do I = 1, N
S₂:            ... B(I,J) ...
        enddo
S₃:        ... C(J) ...
        enddo
```

Notice how the I loop index must be replaced in the statements outside of the inner loop to account for the interchange.

This is useful when loop distribution is not legal, as in the loop:

```
        do I = K+1, N
S₁:        A(I,I) = A(I-1,K+1)  *  A(K,K)
        do J = K+1, N
S₂:            A(I,J)  =  A(I,J)  +  A(I,K)*A(K,J)
        enddo
        enddo
```

The value of $A(I,K)$ that is used in $S_2$ is assigned in $S_1$, and the value of $A(I-1,K+1)$

115

that is used in $S_1$ is assigned on the previous $I$ iteration by $S_2$. Distribution of the $I$ loop would violate the data dependence conditions.

However, it is legal to interchange these loops directly:

```
        do J = K+1, N
S₁:         A(J,J) = A(J-1,K+1) * A(K,K)
            do I = K+1, N
S₂:             A(I,J) = A(I,J) + A(I,K)*A(K,J)
            enddo
        enddo
```

The data dependence relations that are preserved by direct interchanging are:
(a) $S_1[i] \, \delta^* \, S_1[j]$, where $i \leq j$
(b) $S_2[i_1, i_2] \, \delta^* \, S_2[j_1, j_2]$, where $i_1 \leq j_1$ and $i_2 \leq j_2$
(c) $S_1[i] \, \delta^* \, S_2[j_1, j_2]$, where $i \leq j_1$ and $i \leq j_2$
(d) $S_2[i_1, i_2] \, \delta^* \, S_1[j]$, where $i_1 < j$ and $i_2 < j$

Test (a) is obvious and test (b) is the same as the normal loop interchanging test. Test (c) and (d) are similar to data dependence direction vector tests, except that a single loop index, $i$, is being related to both $j_1$ and $j_2$. Test (c) divides the iteration space for $S_2$ into regions, as below:

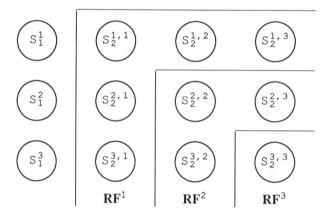

where each region $RF^{i+1}$ is a subset of $RF^i$. Test (c) above means that dependences from $S_1[k]$ to any iteration of $S_2$ in region $RF^k$ will be preserved by direct interchanging, and dependences from $S_1[k]$ to any iteration of $S_2$ outside of region $RF^k$ will be violated.

Test (d) above divides the iteration space into different regions:

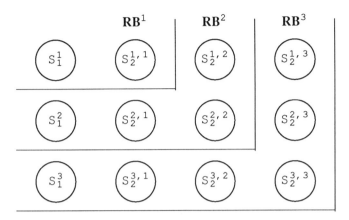

where each region $RB^{i+1}$ is a superset of region $RB^i$. Test (d) means that dependences from any iteration of $S_2$ in region $RB^k$ to $S_1[k+1]$ will be preserved, while dependences from outside of this region to $S_1[k+1]$ will be violated.

The general case also has a statement(s) $S_3$ below the inner loop; direct loop interchanging will preserve dependences:

(e) $S_3[i] \delta^* S_3[j]$, where $i \le j$

(f) $S_1[i] \delta^* S_3[j]$, where $i \le j$

(g) $S_3[i] \delta^* S_1[j]$, where $i < j$

(h) $S_3[i] \delta^* S_2[j_1, j_2]$, where $i < j_1$ and $i < j_2$

(i) $S_2[i_1, i_2] \delta^* S_3[j]$, where $i_1 \le j$ and $i_2 \le j$

Test (e) is obvious, and tests (f) and (g) mean that all dependences between $S_1$ and $S_3$ are preserved. Using the same definition for regions $RF$ and $RB$ in the iteration space of $S_2$, test (h) means that dependences from $S_3[k]$ to any iteration of $S_2$ in region $RF^{k+1}$ will be preserved, and test (i) means that dependences from any iteration of $S_2$ in region $RB^k$ to $S_3[k]$ will be preserved.

Normal direction vector dependence tests are sufficient for conditions (a) and (b), but new dependence tests are needed for (c) and (d). Banerjee's inequalities are not sufficiently flexible, but the Exact Algorithm from Section 2.5.4 can be modified for these purposes. The seventh step of this algorithm accounted for the direction vector; the direction vector relates $i_m$ to $j_m$, or, in terms of the algorithm, $h_{2m-1}$ to $h_{2m}$. Here we want to test to see if there is any dependence with a relation between $i_1$ and $j_1$ and between $i_1$ and $j_2$. In terms of the algorithm, each $i$ and $j$ index corresponds to one of the $h$ variables. Suppose that we are testing only the two loops in question, so that we have only three variables, and we are testing conditions (c) and (d) above, so that:

$$h_1 = i_1, h_2 = j_1, h_3 = j_2$$

Notice that there is no $i_2$; we can either add a dummy $i_2$ with a zero coefficient, or we can reduce the number of $h$ variables. We choose the latter, since the test is exponential in the number of $h$ variables. Condition (c) above will be violated if there is dependence from

$S_1[i]$ to $S_2[j_1, j_2]$ with either $j_1 < i$ or $j_2 < i$. To test for these two relations, in the seventh step of the Exact Algorithm, we first derive the relation:

$$h_2 < h_1$$

and see if dependence still exists; if it does, then condition (c) is violated, and loop interchanging is illegal. Otherwise, we next derive the relation:

$$h_3 < h_1$$

and test again; notice that these two relations must be tested independently, since interchanging is illegal if dependence exists under either relation (which is different than testing for dependence under both relations simultaneously). Similar tests would be used for conditions (d), (h) and (i). Even though the Exact Algorithm may be expensive, it is flexible enough to test for this special kind of optimization.

In the example above, it is easy to see that the dependence relations are:

$$S_1[i] \; \delta \; S_2[i, i] \text{ and } S_2[i, K+1] \; \delta \; S_1[i+1]$$

so that conditions (c) and (d) are both satisfied.

**Triangular Loops.** Testing for this type of loop interchanging is easier when the loop bounds are triangular, as in:

```
          do I = 1, N
S₁:          . . .
             do J = I+1, N
S₂:             . . .
             enddo
          enddo
```

For any iteration of $S_2[i, j]$, the relation $i < j$ is always true. The conditions (c) and (d) for direct interchanging become:

(c') $S_1[i] \; \delta^* \; S_2[j_1, j_2]$, where $i \le j_1$ (since $i \le j_1 < j_2$ implies $i \le j_2$)
(d') $S_2[i_1, i_2] \; \delta^* \; S_1[j]$, where $i_2 < j$ (since $i_1 < i_2 \le j$ implies $i_1 \le j$).
Similar simplifications occur for other types of triangular loop.

**Loop Limits.** All the examples so far have had square or triangular iteration spaces, not general rectangular or trapezoidal. This is for good reason; for square and triangular iteration spaces, after interchanging the new outer loop has the same limits as the old outer loop. Since the statements outside of the inner loop ($S_1$ and $S_3$) must be executed with the old limits, either this restriction must be placed, or conditional statements or other adjustments must be made to ensure proper execution. This is not usually a problem, since in most cases where direct loop interchanging of imperfectly nested loops is legal, either loop distribution is also allowed (and perhaps preferred), or the iteration space is square or triangular, as is the case in many linear algebra algorithms.

## 6.7 Iteration Space Tiling

Block algorithms have been the subject of a great deal of research and study recently. The advantage of block algorithms is that while computing within a block there is a high degree of data reuse, allowing better register, cache or memory hierarchy performance. This research is now well developed enough to include some of the principles in compilers. Previous work in automatically optimizing programs for virtual memory machines [AbuS78, AbKL81] can also be applied to other memory hierarchies. Rather than looking at the algorithm, these optimizations look at the structure of the program and modify the loop structure to produce the same benefits as manual algorithm enhancement. The methods break the iteration space defined by the loop structure into blocks or tiles of some regular shape, and traverse the tiles in an order designed to improve the memory hierarchy utilization.

**Block Algorithms.** Much work has been done on block algorithms with the goal of reducing memory traffic. As an example, the block matrix multiply algorithm is shown here. A basic matrix multiply computes an inner product of a row and a column of matrices B and C for each element of the result matrix A:

```
do I = 1,N
    do J = 1,N
        do K = 1,N
            A(I,J) = A(I,J) + B(I,K)*C(K,J)
        enddo
    enddo
enddo
```

If the arrays are stored columnwise (as in Fortran) in cache lines or pages, then the accesses to B in the loop above will likely refer to a different cache line or page of B in each iteration of the inner loop, causing much unwanted cache or page traffic (unless the cache or memory is large enough to hold the whole B array). The algorithm can be reformulated using subblocks of the arrays:

$$A^{1,1} = B^{1,1}*C^{1,1} + B^{1,2}*C^{2,1}$$
$$A^{1,2} = B^{1,1}*C^{1,2} + B^{1,2}*C^{2,2}$$
$$A^{2,1} = B^{2,1}*C^{1,1} + B^{2,2}*C^{2,1}$$
$$A^{2,2} = B^{2,1}*C^{1,2} + B^{2,2}*C^{2,2}$$

| | | | | | | | |
|---|---|---|---|---|---|---|---|
| $A^{1,1}$ | $A^{1,2}$ | = | $B^{1,1}$ | $B^{1,2}$ | * | $C^{1,1}$ | $C^{1,2}$ |
| $A^{2,1}$ | $A^{2,2}$ | | $B^{2,1}$ | $B^{2,2}$ | | $C^{2,1}$ | $C^{2,2}$ |

This formulation exhibits the advantage that the blocks can be sized to fit into the fastest level of the memory hierarchy, and that during each submatrix multiplication, the data in each sub-matrix is used many times. For this reason, block formulations have been developed for many algorithms. Iteration space tiling tries to duplicate the benefits of block algorithms via program transformations.

**Tiling.** We define *iteration space tiling* as dividing the iteration space into *tiles* (or blocks) of some size and shape (typically squares or cubes), and traversing between the tiles to cover the whole iteration space. Optimal tiling for a memory hierarchy will find tiles such that all the data for each tile will fit into the highest level of the memory hierarchy and will exhibit high data reuse, reducing the total memory traffic. Also, the traversal between tiles will be done in an order that will reduce the amount of data that needs to be moved when going to the next tile.

Tiling is also a good paradigm for multiprocessor computers. If tiling can be done so that different tiles are independent of each other, then different tiles can be assigned to different processors. The data locality of tiling will also help multiprocessors by reducing memory contention.

Tiling can be implemented by a combination of strip mining and loop interchanging. Strip mining divides each loop into strips; each loop becomes two loops:

```
do I = 1, N
```

becomes

```
do IT = 1, N, IS
do I = IT, MIN(N,IT+IS-1)
```

We call **do** IT the "tile loop", and **do** I the "element loop", since **do** IT traverses between tiles and **do** I traverses between elements of the iteration space. The tile size, IS, may be different for each loop in a loop nest, since tiles need not be square. Simple minded strip mining of each loop would produce the following code for a matrix multiply:

```
do IT = 1, N, IS
do I = IT, MIN(N, IT+IS-1)
   do JT = 1, N, JS
   do J = JT, MIN(N, JT+JS-1)
      do KT = 1, N, KS
      do K = KT, MIN(N, KT+KS-1)
         A(I,J)=A(I,J)+B(I,K)*C(K,J)
```

Loop interchanging is then used to move the tile loops outwards and the element loops inwards:

```
do IT = 1, N, IS
do JT = 1, N, JS
do KT = 1, N, KS
    do I = IT, MIN(N, IT+IS-1)
    do J = JT, MIN(N, JT+JS-1)
    do K = KT, MIN(N, KT+KS-1)
        A(I,J)=A(I,J)+B(I,K)*C(K,J)
```

In the example of matrix multiply, the loops can easily be interchanged; in the general case, the loops cannot always be interchanged. In those cases, automatic iteration space tiling may not produce an optimal program.

The final step is to optimize the order of the tile and element loops. The tile loops should be ordered so that the tiles are traversed in such a way as to reduce the amount of data moved between tiles. For instance, the tile loop ordering shown above refers to different blocks of B and C for each iteration of the KT loop:

```
do IT = 1, N, IS
do JT = 1, N, JS
    load block A^{IT,JT}
    do KT = 1, N, KS
        load blocks B^{IT,KT}, C^{KT,JT}
        compute A^{IT,JT} = A^{IT,JT} + B^{IT,KT} * C^{KT,JT}
    enddo
    store block A^{IT,JT}
enddo
enddo
```

Each block of A is loaded and stored only once, while the B and C blocks are loaded multiple times (N/JS loads of each B block and N/IS loads of each C block). For computers with private memories on each processor, explicit data moves must be added in the code. For computers with hardware-managed caches, the data motion will be done automatically, though the same data motion patterns will apply. A different tile loop ordering has different characteristics:

```
do IT = 1, N, IS
do KT = 1, N, KS
    load block B^{IT,KT}
    do JT = 1, N, JS
        load blocks A^{IT,JT}, C^{KT,JT}
        compute A^{IT,JT} = A^{IT,JT} + B^{IT,KT} * C^{KT,JT}
        store block A^{IT,JT}
    enddo
enddo
enddo
```

This tile loop ordering requires multiple loads and stores of the blocks of A, while reducing the number of loads required for each block of B. Generally, the first tile loop ordering would be preferable for most systems; if for some reason loading a block of B was expensive, the second tile loop ordering may be more effective. Tiling of the iteration space creates a tiling or blocking of the data arrays. The order in which the tiles are traversed induces the order in which the data blocks are accessed.

Another consideration is the concurrency in the algorithm, for multiprocessor computers. In general, it is more efficient to make outer loops concurrent (instead of inner loops) due to reduced overhead cost of forking and joining.

The element loop ordering must also be optimized. For vector computers, the element loops should ordered so that the inner loop is vectorizable, with appropriate memory strides (most vector computers work best with unit stride memory fetches). The element loop ordering may be important even for non-vector computers; when the loops can be ordered to increase the loop invariant computation or memory addresses in the inner loop, more code floating or better register assignment may be possible by the compiler.

**Tiling of a Non-Square Iteration Space.** Using simple minded strip mining to tile the triangular loops below:

```
do I = 1, N
    do J = I, N
```

may produce the wrong result. The desired tiling pattern for the two dimensional triangular loop is:

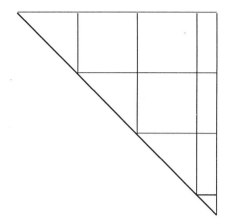

However, simple minded strip mining cannot generate this pattern. The proper way to strip mine the loops is:

```
do IT = 1, N, IS
do JT = IT, N, IS
    do I = IT, MIN(N,IT+IS-1)
    do J = MAX(JT,I), MIN(N,JT+IS-1)
```

Note that this produces some triangular tiles (along the diagonal) and some square tiles (throughout the rest of the iteration space). Note also that the tile size must be the same for both loops. For a triply-nested triangular loop, the situation gets even more complicated:

```
do K = 1, N
    do I = K, N
        do J = K, N
```

can be tiled to:

```
do KT = 1, N, KS
do IT = KT, N, KS
do JT = KT, N, KS
    do K = KT, MIN(N, KT+KS-1)
    do I = MAX(K,IT),MIN(N,IT+KS-1)
    do J = MAX(K,JT),MIN(N,JT+KS-1)
```

The original iteration space is a right pyramid; the tiled iteration space produces some right pyramid tiles, some wedge tiles and some cube tiles. Triangular loops may arise naturally (many linear algebra algorithms use triangular loops) or through other program transformations (such as loop skewing, Chapter 8).

# 7 Reductions and Recurrences

Recognition of and efficient code generation for reduction operations is important in vector and concurrent loops, due to their frequency. Reduction recognition was already mentioned in Chapters 3 and 4; here we discuss the problems of roundoff error accumulation that must be faced when dealing with reduction operations.

Another problem facing a supercomputer architect is how to execute recurrence relations fast. A recurrence relation is by its very nature a non-parallel construct and is generally expressed in sequential terms. Fast methods for solving recurrence relations have been designed [ChKu75], [SaBr77]. These methods change the recurrence solving algorithm into one which exhibits much parallelism. The cost of using these methods is that sometimes a great deal of hardware is required and computational redundancy inserted by the methods appears in the results as increased round-off error. Recurrences can sometimes be avoided (by interchanging loops, perhaps), but genuine arithmetic recurrences do appear in source programs and need to be executed - quickly if possible and serially if necessary.

The most common form of arithmetic recurrence relation is the first order linear recurrence. Studying this class of recurrence is interesting since it is the only kind of recurrence for which hardware has yet been built. This chapter will study various forms of the first order linear recurrence and how they are affected by the appearance of **if** statements. The next chapter studies a new formulation of the wavefront method for solving recurrences with two dimensional data.

## 7.1 Roundoff Error in Reductions

As mentioned in Chapter 3, a reduction appears in the dependence graph as a cycle. Thus, the loop:

```
        do I = 1, N
S₁:       S = S + A(I)
        enddo
```

has the dependence graph:

A vectorizing compiler will inspect this cycle, recognize the summation, and generate the code:

```
S₁:  S = S + SUM(A(1:N))
```

Vectorizing arithmetic reductions (such as SUM, PRODUCT and DOTPRODUCT) can produce different answers due to different roundoff error accumulation. For instance, while most computers have an instruction or an algorithm to accumulate SUM reductions, they usually work by accumulating some number of partial sums (the sum of every $r$th number) and then adding up the partial sums. Since computer floating point arithmetic is not truly associative, the final answers may be somewhat different. On a machine such as the Cyber 205, where the number of vector pipelines may differ from one installation to the next, the answers may be different for different installations. The Cyber 205 also accumulates SUM reductions in unnormalized double precision floating point, so not only is the order of the additions different, but a different computer arithmetic is used.

Some of these effects may turn out to produce a "better" answer on average, but nonetheless the answer will be different from the original scalar program. Indeed, in one experiment, we had vectorized a program for the Cyber 205, but found that one answer had changed in sign from the original program. We eventually tracked the difference to roundoff error accumulation differences for a SUM reduction; as it turned out, the magnitude of the answer was $10^{-17}$, so the whole answer was nothing but accumulated roundoff error. However, to prevent users from getting different answers, many compilers now have a switch controlling whether roundoff error changing optimizations can be performed. If the switch is reset, then arithmetic reductions are not vectorized. Notice that non-arithmetic reductions do not suffer from problems with roundoff error differences, such as:

```
do I = 1, N
    AMAX = MAX( AMAX, A(I) )
enddo
```

which can be converted to:

```
AMAX = MAX( AMAX, MAXVAL(A(1:N)) )
```

Roundoff error can accumulate differently in concurrentized loops also. If the summation above were translated into a concurrent loop, each processor would accumulate its own partial sum, and then the final result would be combined at the bottom of the loop:

```
doall p = 1,  numberP
    SX (p) = 0
    do I = p, N, numberP
        SX (p) = SX (p) + A (I)
    enddo
    enter critical region
    S = S + SX (p)
    exit critical region
enddo
```

The sample code above also used prescheduling. If a self-scheduling were used, then the program may assign iterations differently each time the program is run; this means that the program may get a slightly different answer for the same data. The Alliant compiler, which can generate this type of code automatically, has a command line switch to control this optimization. If *dynamic reassociation* is allowed (by the user), then the compiler has the freedom to generate self-scheduled concurrent reductions; the program may get different answers each time it is run. If only *static reassociation* is allowed, the compiler must generate code that will give the same answer each time the program is run, regardless of the number of processors available. If no reassociation is allowed, then the code must give the same answer as the serial program would have; in this case, recognition of concurrent reductions is enabled only for those nonarithmetic reductions that do not display roundoff error problems, such as finding the MAX or MIN of a vector.

**Interchanging Around Reductions.** Strictly speaking, the dependence relations for a two-dimensional reduction, such as:

```
        do I = 1, N
            do J = 1, M
S₁:             S = S + A(I,J)
            enddo
        enddo
```

are:

$$S_1 \, \delta^*_{(\le, \, *)} \, S_1$$

In particular, the condition $S_1 \, \delta_{(<, \, <)} \, S_1$ holds, meaning that loop interchanging is illegal. However, as is the case with vectorization and concurrentization, reduction operations can be handled specially. If arithmetic reassociation is allowed (by the user), then the reduction operation can be interchanged:

```
        do J = 1, M
            do I = 1, N
S₁:             S = S + A(I,J)
            enddo
        enddo
```

The advantages may be longer loop limits or stride-1 array accesses; in either case, the interchanged loop will accumulate the reduction differently than the original loop, so this optimization should be performed only when the user allows it. As mentioned earlier, nonarithmetic reductions do not suffer from roundoff error accumulation, and so loops with only these reductions can be interchanged without worry.

**Coupled Reductions.** A relatively infrequent but occasionally important construct is two reductions into the same variable:

```
do I = 1, N
    A(I) = B(I) + C(I)
    S = S + A(I)
    D(I) = E(I) + F(I)
    S = S + D(I)
enddo
```

The dependence graph for this loop has the two reductions coupled in a tight dependence cycle. As long as reassociation is allowed by the user and the reductions are conformable, the two reduction statements can be treated (vectorized, concurrentized, etc.) independently:

```
A(1:N) = B(1:N) + C(1:N)
S = S + SUM( A(1:N) )
D(1:N) = E(1:N) + F(1:N)
S = S + SUM( D(1:N) )
```

## 7.2 First Order Linear Arithmetic Recurrences

There are many forms of the first order linear arithmetic recurrence. The general form is:

```
do I = 2, N
    X(I) = X(I-1)*A(I) + C(I)
enddo
```

The initial condition (X(1)), the coefficient vector (A) and the constant vector (C) are inputs to the recurrence. A program for solving this recurrence with array operations using N parallel processors is shown below:

```
X(2:N) = C(2:N)
do M = 0, CEIL(LOG2(N)) - 1
    J = 2**M
    X(J+1:N) = X(J+1:N) + X(1:N-J)*A(J+1:N)
    A(J+1:N) = A(J+1:N)*A(1:N-J)
enddo
```

This is the algorithm given in [SaBr77] for the special case of the first order recurrence, modified to use no broadcasts.

An important variant of the basic first order linear recurrence is the "constant-coefficient" case, when all the elements of the coefficient vector (A) are equal, or when the coefficient is a scalar:

```
do I = 2, N
    X(I) = X(I-1)*A + C(I)
enddo
```

The corresponding parallel algorithm is:

```
X(2:N)  = C(2:N)
do M = 0, CEIL(LOG2(N)) - 1
    J = 2**M
    X(J+1:N) = X(J+1:N) + X(1:N-J)*A
    A = A*A
enddo
```

The special case where $A = 1$ is a trivial extension of this case.

Another important variant is the "remote-term" case, when the recurrence variable (X) is a scalar:

```
do I = 2, N
    X = X*A(I) + C(I)
enddo
```

Solving this recurrence in parallel requires progressively fewer operations in each parallel step:

```
Y(1) = X
Y(2:N) = C(2:N)
do M = 0, CEIL(LOG2(N)) - 1
    J = 2**M
    JJ = 2*J
    Y(JJ:N:JJ) = Y(JJ:N:JJ) + Y(JJ:N-J:JJ)*A(JJ:N:JJ)
    A(JJ:N:JJ) = A(JJ:N:JJ)*A(J:N-J:JJ)
enddo
X = Y(N)
```

Upon finding an alternate form of a recurrence, the compiler may be able to rewrite it into a standard form. For instance, the following loop is a first order linear recurrence but it is not in the standard form:

```
do I = 2, N
    X(I) = (X(I-1) + B(I)) * A(I)
enddo
```

By applying arithmetic distribution of multiplication over addition, it can be changed into normal form:

```
C(2:N) = B(2:N) * A(2:N)
do I = 2, N
    X(I) = X(I-1) * A(I) + C(I)
enddo
```

**Roundoff Error.** All these parallel algorithms for solving linear recurrences have different roundoff error accumulation characteristics than the original serial algorithm. In particular, since some of the parallel algorithms perform more operations then the serial algorithm, the roundoff error accumulation for the parallel algorithm may be more severe and may give bad answers for ill-conditioned problems.

Some compilers recognize standard recurrence forms and replace these by calls to numerical library routines, which have been tuned for speed and numerical accuracy. Even in these cases, performing reassociation or distribution to change the form of a recurrence to fit into the mold of the numerical library routine will change the roundoff error characteristics.

**IF Statements.** Conditional recurrences can be handled by either changing them into unconditional recurrences, or by modifying the parallel algorithm to allow conditionals. The conditional recurrence in Figure 7.1(a) can be changed into normal form by using compiler temporary arrays and masked moves, as in Figure 7.1(b).

```
do I = 2, N
    if( TEST(I) ) X(I) = X(I-1)*A(I) + C(I)
enddo
```

```
        (a)
```

```
where( TEST(2:N) ) do
    AA(2:N) = A(2:N)
    CC(2:N) = C(2:N)
elsewhere
    AA(2:N) = 0
    CC(2:N) = X(2:N)
endwhere
do I = 2, N
    X(I) = X(I-1)*AA(I) + CC(I)
enddo
```

```
        (b)
```

**Figure 7.1.** Conditional recurrence. (a) Serial form of conditional recurrence. (b) Conditional recurrence changed into normal form by using compiler temporary variables.

This is not really necessary however, since the parallel recurrence algorithm itself can be modified to use the mask vector as another input. The effect of the **if** test can be implemented without the extra memory and move time. The modified recurrence algorithm which uses an input mask vector is:

```
where ( TEST (2:N) ) X (2:N) = C (2:N)
do M = 0, CEIL (LOG2 (N)) - 1
    J = 2**M
    where ( TEST (J:N) ) do
        X (J+1:N) = X (J+1:N) + X (1:N-J) *A (J+1:N)
        A (J+1:N) = A (J+1:N) *A (1:N-J)
    endwhere
    TEST (J+1:N) = TEST (J+1:N) and TEST (1:N-J)
enddo
```

The same technique does not work for the remote term case, however. The conditional remote term recurrence below:

```
do I = 2, N
    if ( TEST (I) ) X = X * A (I) + C (I)
enddo
```

computes the last term of the following general-term recurrence:

```
do I = 2, N
    if ( TEST (I) ) then
        X (I) = X (I-1) * A (I) + C (I)
    else
        X (I) = X (I-1)
    endif
enddo
```

not the last term of the simpler conditional general-term recurrence in Figure 7.1(a). The conditional remote term case can be solved with the use of compiler temporary arrays and vector operations:

```
where ( TEST (2:N) ) do
    AA (2:N) = A (2:N)
    CC (2:N) = C (2:N)
elsewhere
    AA (2:N) = 1
    CC (2:N) = 0
endwhere
do I = 2, N
    X = X*AA (I) + CC (I)
enddo
```

Notice the difference between this and Figure 7.1(b).

## 7.3 Postfix IFs

Not all dependence cycles are arithmetic recurrences. A certain class of data/control dependence cycles includes **if** statements and is called Postfix ifs. An example of a Postfix **if** is shown in Figure 7.2(a). This loop can be transformed into the parallel code in Figure 7.2(b), where $S_1$–$S_4$ and $S_9$–$S_{10}$ are vector statements, and $S_5$–$S_8$ are a special form of boolean recurrence which can be solved by a special piece of hardware:

---

```
do I = 2, N
    if ( X(I-1) > 0 ) then
        X(I) = G(I) + H(I)
    else
        X(I) = E(I) * F(I)
    endif
enddo
```

(a)

```
S₁:  X1(2:N)  = G(2:N) + H(2:N)
S₂:  X2(2:N)  = E(2:N) * F(2:N)
S₃:  B1(3:N)  = X1(2:N-1) > 0
S₄:  B2(3:N)  = X2(2:N-1) > 0
S₅:  C1(2)    = X(1) > 0
S₆:  C2(2)    = not C1(2)
     do I = 3, N
S₇:      C1(I) = (C1(I-1) and B1(I)) or (C2(I-1) and B2(I))
S₈:      C2(I) = (C1(I-1) and not B1(I)) or (C2(I-1) and not B2(I))
     enddo
S₉:  where ( C1(2:N) ) X(2:N) = X1(2:N)
S₁₀: where ( C2(2:N) ) X(2:N) = X2(2:N)
```

(b)

**Figure 7.2.** Postfix **if** in a loop. (a) Serial form of a two-way Postfix **if**. (b) Parallel code for a Postfix **if**.

---

We start with a general discussion of the execution of loops with Postfix **ifs**. A Postfix **if** is characterized by having an **if** test that chooses between two (or more) statements (or sequences of statements), one or more of which is an assignment to a variable which will be tested in a later iteration by the **if**. There is a dependence cycle involving a control dependence from the **if** to some conditional assignment, and a data flow-dependence from the assignment back to the **if**. To make rules concerning the classification of **ifs**, we will study Figure 7.2 in detail.

In Figure 7.2(b), statements $S_1$ and $S_2$ "precompute" the values of the recurrence variable $X$ into compiler temporary arrays for each path of the **if**. By this we mean that the right hand side expressions of the assignments to the recurrence variable are computed (for the whole index set of the loop) and saved in temporary arrays. After the execution of the loop, each $X(I)$ will be one of $X1(I)$ or $X2(I)$. Statements $S_3$ and $S_4$ precompute the values of the **if** test for each possible previous path of the **if** test. Statements $S_5$ and $S_6$ initialize the boolean recurrence, and $S_7$ and $S_8$ solve it. After the recurrence, the boolean variables $C1$ and $C2$ hold the proper values of the **if** test. These variables are used to mask the assignments of the precomputed values into the recurrence variable in statements $S_9$ and $S_{10}$.

Notice that in this example $C1$ and $C2$ are complements of each other, so actually only one of these is needed. For multi-way branches, there would be one $C$ variable for each branch, or more precisely, one $C$ variable for each possible value of the recurrence variable(s).

Two important points define Postfix **if**s. First, the values of the recurrence variable must be pre-computable. Second, the boolean recurrence must be simple enough to solve. This last concept is purposely vague, since it is driven by the complexity of the hardware needed to solve the recurrence; more difficult recurrence forms require more complicated hardware for fast solution. Towle [Towl76] defines a special class of Postfix **if**s, called B-postfix **if**s, as those which can be solved with a linear coupled boolean recurrence; by linear we mean that no two recurrence variable can be "ANDed" in the recurrence. He gives a complicated set of conditions which must be satisfied for the **if** to be classified as B-postfix. This is an arbitrary restriction to simplify the kind of hardware needed to solve the boolean recurrence.

Focusing on the form of the boolean recurrence of the B-postfix **if**, we see that it looks like:

**do** $I$ = *distance* to N
    **do** P = 1 to *paths*
$$C(P,I) = \sum_{Q=1}^{paths} C(Q,I-distance) \textbf{ and } "TEST(Q,I) = 'take\ path\ P'$$
    **enddo**
**enddo**

or, in English, "take path $P$ in iteration $I$ if for any $Q$, we took path $Q$ in iteration '$I$ - *distance*' and the **if** test using the data from path $Q$ says to take path $P$."

Note that the *distance* is a fixed constant. A loop containing a Postfix **if** but with a non-fixed distance (see Figure 7.3(a)) can be transformed into Postfix code (see Figure 7.3(b)). However, the boolean recurrence is not in simple B-postfix form, and thus is too complicated for a B-postfix boolean recurrence solver. With a more complicated hardware boolean recurrence solver, this type of recurrence would be acceptable. The techniques in [BaGK80] can be used to build such hardware.

```
do I = 2 to N
    if ( X(I-1) > X(I-2) ) then
        X(I) = G(I) + H(I)
    else
        X(I) = E(I) * F(I)
    endif
enddo
```

(a)

```
S₁: X1(2:N) = G(2:N) + H(2:N)
S₂: X2(2:N) = E(2:N) * F(2:N)

S₃: B11(4:N) = X1(3:N-1) > X1(2:N-2)
S₄: B12(4:N) = X1(3:N-1) > X2(2:N-2)
S₅: B21(4:N) = X2(3:N-1) > X1(2:N-2)
S₆: B22(4:N) = X2(3:N-1) > X2(2:N-2)

S₇: C1(2) = X(1) > X(0)
S₈: C1(3) = C1(2) and X1(2) > X(1) or
            not C1(2) and X2(2) > X(1)
    do I = 4, N
S₉:     C1(I) = (C1(I-1) and C1(I-2) and B11(I)) or
                (C1(I-1) and not C1(I-2) and B12(I)) or
                (not C1(I-1) and C1(I-2) and B21(I)) or
                (not C1(I-1) and not C1(I-2) and B22(I))
    enddo
S₁₀: where ( C1(2:N) ) X(2:N) = X1(2:N)
S₁₁: where ( not C1(2:N) ) X(2:N) = X2(2:N)
```

**Figure 7.3.** Postfix **if** with non-fixed distance. (a) Original loop, with dependence cycle with dependence distances of 1 and 2. (b) Parallel Postfix form of the loop; notice that the boolean recurrence in $S_9$ is much more complicated than in Figure 7.2(b).

The complexity of the boolean recurrence depends on two factors: the number of paths of the **if** and the number of dependence distances. The number of paths affects the number of variables in the recurrence; there are as many variables (and assignments) in the recurrence as there are paths of the **if**. Also, the number of paths affects the number of minterms in each assignment. The number of dependence distances affects the complexity of each minterm in each assignment and the number of minterms; the number of minterms in each assignment is num-paths$^{\text{num-distances}}$; the number of boolean recurrence "C" variables ANDed together in each minterm is num-distances.

Postfix **ifs** can have more than one recurrence variable, as in the loop below. The method of solution is similar to the one-variable case:

```
do I = 2, N
    if ( X(I-1) > Y(I-1) then
        X(I) = ...
        Y(I) = ...
    else
        X(I) = ...
        Y(I) = ...
    endif
enddo
```

Since the dependence distance is the same for both variables, this example is B-postfix.

Precomputation of the values of the recurrence variable is possible if and only if there are no data dependence arcs $S_v \, \delta_{(<)} \, S_w$ in the cycle containing the **if**, except where $S_w$ is the **if** test itself. For example, the following loop:

```
      do I = 2 to N
S₁:       if ( X(I-1) > 0 ) then
S₂:           X(I) = E(I)
          else
S₃:           X(I) = X(I-1)*2 - T
          endif
      enddo
```

is not a Postfix **if** since the data dependence relations

$$S_2 \, \delta_{(<)} \, S_3 \text{ and } S_3 \, \delta_{(<)} \, S_3$$

both exist. In the canonical Postfix **if**, each element of the recurrence variable had only two possible values, which could be easily precomputed. In this example, each element of the recurrence variable has many possible values:

```
X(2) = E(2)
    or X(1)*2-T

X(3) = E(3)
    or X(2)*2-T = E(2)*2-T
                or (X(1)*2-T)*2-T

X(4) = E(4)
    or X(3)*2-T = E(3)*2-T
                or (X(2)*2-T)*2-T = (E(2)*2-T)*2-T
                                 or ((X(1)*2-T)*2-T)*2-T
```

· · ·

In fact, for X(I) there are I possible values. Precomputing all these requires precomputing $\frac{N(N-1)}{2}$ values, and the entire process would become more complicated than the solution of a Postfix **if**.

# 8 Wavefronts via Loop Skewing

Occasionally a multi-dimensional loop will be encountered where loop interchanging cannot be used to find a parallel loop. One example of such a loop is a four point difference operation:

```
    do I = 2, N-1
        do J = 2, M-1
S₁:         A(I,J) = (A(I-1,J) + A(I+1,J)
                    + A(I,J-1) + A(I,J+1))/4
        enddo
    enddo
```

The iteration space dependence graph for this loop is:

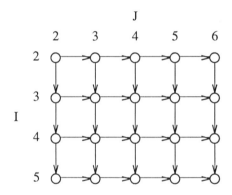

It is easily seen that the inner loop cannot be executed in parallel. Moreover, even though the loops can be interchanged, the new inner loop will not be a parallel loop either. Parallelism can be found in cases like this, with the *wavefront method* ([Mura71, Lamp74, Kuhn80]). Here we give an alternate formulation of the wavefront method based on *loop skewing* and loop interchanging.

## 8.1 Loop Skewing

We skew a loop index J with respect to index I by a factor of $f$ (where $f$ is an integer greater than one) by
(a) replacing the lower loop limit of the J loop, LBJ, with the expression LBJ+I*$f$,
(b) replacing the upper loop limit of the J loop, UBJ with the expression UBJ+I*$f$, and
(c) replacing all occurrences of J in the loop with the expression J−I*$f$.
    After skewing the J loop of the four point difference operation, we get:

```
        do I = 2, N-1
           do J = I+2, I+M-1
S₁:              A(I,J-I) = (A(I-1,J-I) + A(I+1,J-I)
                            + A(I,J-I-1) + A(I,J-I+1))/4
           enddo
        enddo
```

The new iteration space is also skewed:

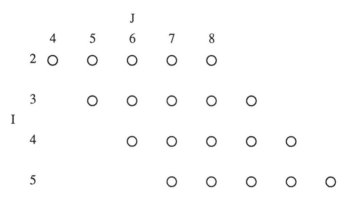

Loop skewing is always legal; it has no effect on the numerical results of the program. It does not even change the execution order of the iterations (iterations in the skewed iteration space are executed in the same order as the corresponding iterations in the original iteration space). It does affect the data dependence direction vectors.

*Example.* Suppose we have a data dependence direction vector of $(<, =)$, and we skew the inner loop with respect to the outer loop by a factor of one. The new direction vector must relate $S_v[i_1, i_2+i_1] \delta^* S_w[j_1, j_2+j_2]$. The first element in the direction vector does not change, but the second element will relate:

$$i_2+i_1 \; \psi'_2 \; j_2+j_1$$

Since the original direction vector implied:

$$i_1 < j_1 \text{ and } i_2 = j_2$$

this means that $\psi'_2$ must be $(<)$.

Thus, skewing by a factor of one will change any $(<,=)$ directions to $(<,<)$ directions. In general, if there was a dependence relation $S_v[i_1, i_2] \delta^* S_w[j_1, j_2]$ in the original loop, then after loop skewing, the dependence relation is changed to $S_v[i_1, i_2+f*i_1] \delta^* S_w[j_1, j_2+f*j_2]$. If the original data dependence direction vector was $(\psi_1, \psi_2)$, the modified direction vector is $(\psi_1, \psi'_2)$, (only the element corresponding to the skewed loop changes). If the skew factor is positive, then $\psi'_2 = \text{SHIFT}(\psi_1, \psi_2)$, where SHIFT is defined:

| SHIFT | $\psi_2$ | | | |
|---|---|---|---|---|
| | < | = | > | * |
| $\psi_1$ < | < | < | ? | * |
| = | < | = | > | * |
| > | ? | > | > | * |
| * | * | * | * | * |

Question marks in the table mean that the value of SHIFT cannot be determined from the direction vector alone. The entries are derived as shown in the example above.

We can see the effects of index set skewing by looking at the iteration space dependence graph of the skewed four point difference operation:

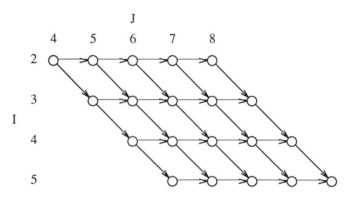

Note that SHIFT(<,>) and SHIFT(<,>) are indeterminate. If we know more than the information in the data dependence direction vector, then we may be able to find the value of SHIFT in particular cases.

**Lemma 8.1.**

Let the minimum distance $d_k^{min}$ and maximum distance $d_k^{max}$ be defined such that for all $\bar{i} = (i_1, \ldots, i_d)$ and $\bar{j} = (j_1, \ldots, j_d)$ such that $S_v[\bar{i}] \ \delta^* \ S_w[\bar{j}]$, the relation $d_k^{min} \leq j_k - i_k \leq d_k^{max}$ holds. If we skew index $i_k$ with respect to index $i_m$ by a factor $f$, then the modified direction vector element $\psi_k$ is:

$\psi_k \equiv (<)$, if $f*d_m^{min} > -d_k^{min}$
$\psi_k \equiv (>)$, if $f*d_m^{max} < -d_k^{max}$
$\psi_k \equiv (=)$, if $f*d_m^{min} = f*d_m^{max} = -d_k^{min} = -d_k^{max}$

**Proof.**

For any index set values $\bar{i}, \bar{j}$ such that $S_v[\bar{i}] \ \delta^* \ S_w[\bar{j}]$, we have

$$d_m^{min} \leq j_m - i_m \leq d_m^{max} \text{ and } d_m^{min} \leq j_k - i_k \leq d_k^{max}$$

The modified direction vector element $\psi_k$ will satisfy:

$$f*i_m + i_k \ \psi_k \ f*j_m + j_k, \text{ or}$$
$$0 \ \psi_k \ f*(j_m-i_m) + j_k-i_k$$

If $f*d_m^{min} > -d_k^{min}$, then

$$f*(j_m-i_m) + j_k-i_k \geq f*d_m^{min} + d_k^{min} > 0$$
so, $\psi_k \equiv (<)$.

If $f*d_m^{max} < -d_k^{max}$, then

$$f*(j_m-i_m) + j_k-i_k \leq f*d_m^{max} + d_k^{max} < 0$$
so, $\psi_k \equiv (>)$.

If $f*d_m^{min} = f*d_m^{max} = -d_k^{min} = -d_k^{min}$, then

$$f*(j_m-i_m) + j_k-i_k = f*d_m^{min} + d_k^{min} = 0$$
so, $\psi_k \equiv (=)$.

The values of $d^{min}$ and $d^{max}$ can be derived from the exact decision algorithms for data dependence testing.

## 8.2 Interchanging with Skewed Index Sets

After skewing index sets, we may be able to interchange the loops. The same rules for interchanging loops that were given in Chapter 6 apply here; the only special detail is how to handle the loop limits. To interchange loops of the form

```
do I = LBI to UBI
    do J = f*I + LBJ to f*I + UBJ
```

where `LBJ` and `UBJ` are expressions that do not depend on `I` the loop limits are changed to:

```
do J = f*LBI + LBJ, f*UBI + UBJ
    do I = MAX(LBI, CEIL((J-UBJ)/f)), MIN(UBI, CEIL((J-LBJ)/f)
```

This is a generalization of interchanging trapezoidal loops, as discussed in Chapter 6.

After skewing the loops for the four point difference operation, we can interchange the two loops to get:

```
        do J = 4, M+N-2
            do I = MAX(2,J-M+1), MIN(N-1,J-2)
S₁:             A(I,J-I) = (A(I-1,J-I) + A(I+1,J-I)
                          + A(I,J-I-1) + A(I,J-I+1))/4
            enddo
        enddo
```

The process of skewing index sets and interchanging loops can be repeated if there are more than 2 loops in the loop nest. For example, in a three dimensional six-point difference operation, such as:

```
        do I = 2, N-1
            do J = 2, M-1
                do K = 2, P-1
S₁:                 A(I,J,K) = (A(I-1,J,K) + A(I+1,J,K)
                        + A(I,J-1,K) + A(I,J+1,K)
                        + A(I,J,K-1) + A(I,J,K+1))/4
            enddo
        enddo
```

we can skew index K with respect to both indices I and J (by factors of 1), resulting in:

```
        do I = 2, N-1
            do J = 2, M-1
                do K = I+J+2, I+J+P-1
S₁:                 A(I,J,K-I-J) = (A(I-1,J,K-I-J) + A(I+1,J,K-I-J)
                        + A(I,J-1,K-I-J) + A(I,J+1,K-I-J)
                        + A(I,J,K-I-J-1) + A(I,J,K-I-J+1))/4
            enddo
        enddo
```

After interchanging the **do** K loop to the outermost position, the loop would look like:

```
        do K = 6, N+M+P-3
            do I = MAX(2,K-M-P), MIN(N-1,K-4)
                do J = MAX(2,K-I-P), MIN(M-1,K-I-2)
S₁:                 A(I,J,K-I-J) = (A(I-1,J,K-I-J) + A(I+1,J,K-I-J)
                        + A(I,J-1,K-I-J) + A(I,J+1,K-I-J)
                        + A(I,J,K-I-J-1) + A(I,J,K-I-J+1))/4
            enddo
        enddo
```

## 8.3 Parallelism with Index Set Skewing

We can uncover parallelism by index set skewing. For instance, in the original four point difference operation, neither loop could be executed in parallel. After skewing the index set and interchanging the loops the **do** I loop can be executed in parallel for all values of its index set, if the **do** J loop is executed serially.

This is possible because skewing the index set modifies the data dependence direction vectors. By skewing the index set of the innermost loop, we can change the corresponding entry of all data dependence direction vectors to a forward $(<)$ direction. Then we can interchange this loop to the outermost position. Finally, if we execute this loop serially, then all the data dependence relations will be satisfied, and all the other loops can be executed in parallel.

140

Index set skewing should only be used when loop interchanging and loop vectorization do not produce enough parallelism in the loop. Index set skewing results in triangular loops (which start out with short vectors) and complicated array indexing patterns which may not execute well on many machines.

Skewing by large factors produces inefficient programs. We expect that most applications that need skewing will use factors of one or two. One class of loops can be shown to need only a factor of one.

**Lemma 8.2.**

If we have a d-dimensional loop, and all data dependence relations have directions vectors $\Psi = (\psi_1, \ldots, \psi_d)$, where either

$$\psi_1 \equiv \psi_2 \equiv \cdots \equiv \psi_d \equiv \, =, \text{ or}$$
$$\psi_j \in \{=, <, \leq\}, \text{ forall } j, \text{ and some } \psi_k \equiv <$$

Then

1) we can skew index $I_d$ (the innermost loop) with respect to $I_1, I_2, \ldots, I_{d-1}$ by a factor of one,
2) we can interchange the $I_d$ loop to the outermost position, and
3) executing the $I_d$ loop serially allows parallel execution of all the other loops.

**Proof.**

Skewing the index sets as given is always legal, so there is no problem there. The skew will change the data dependence direction vectors as follows:

$$S_v \, \delta_{(=, =, \ldots, =)} \, S_w \text{ will remain the same;}$$
$$S_v \, \delta_{(\psi_1, \ldots, <, \ldots, \psi_d)} \, S_w \text{ will become } S_v \, \delta_{(\psi_1, \ldots, <, \ldots, <)} \, S_w;$$
$$S_v \, \delta_{(=, =, \ldots, <)} \, S_w \text{ will remain the same.}$$

Thus, except for all-equal direction vectors, all direction vectors will have a forward direction in $\psi_d$. Interchanging the $I_d$ index to the outermost position is legal since there is no data dependence relation in the modified loop with a backwards directions in any position. Now executing the **do** $I_d$ loop serially will satisfy all data dependence relations (except those with all-equal directions) and all the other loops can be executed in parallel.

This is shown informally in [Wolf78]

## 8.4 Comparison with the Wavefront Method

The method given here of skewing index sets and interchanging loops is equivalent to the wavefront method [Mura71, Lamp74, Kuhn80]. Direct analogies can be drawn between "finding the critical angle" in [Kuhn80] and finding $d^{max}$ and $d^{min}$ here. We have attempted to generalize whenever possible.

We did not go into details of finding $d^{max}$ and $d^{min}$ In some cases, the exact decision algorithms of Chapter 2 may be applicable, since they can return the entire subset of the index set that causes the dependence. The Data Arc Set method in [Kuhn80] is also applicable. In any case, computing $d^{max}$ and $d^{min}$ is required only when the SHIFT function cannot be used; using the data dependence direction vectors can reduce the amount of time spent in the more complicated dependence test necessary to find $d^{max}$ and $d^{min}$.

**Supernode Partitioning.** *Supernode Partitioning* [IrTr88] divides an iteration space into nodes with several goals: vector computation within a node, data reuse within a tile, and parallelism between tiles. It can also be derived as a combination of three transformations: loop skewing (to modify the iteration space before tiling), iteration space tiling and concurrentization of the tile loops.

# 9 Storage Management

A compiler creates many temporary variables in the course of compiling a program. Temporary variables are used to hold subexpression values, addresses and other values for which no explicit variable was specified by the programmer. Managing these compiler-generated variables is a well-known art. Wise management and judicious register assignment can keep the number of actual memory locations needed for compiler temporary variables at a minimum. When compiling a standard language for a serial machine, the most that the compiler will use is some (small) number of scalar storage locations.

When compiling programs for array-oriented machines, compiler-generated array temporaries will be required. Given the array semantics of the proposed new standard Fortran language (Fortran 8x [ANSI87]), an array expression can be written that requires an array temporary even when compiled for a serial machine. While it is easy and inexpensive to add a few compiler temporary scalars, creating temporary arrays can cause problems. The first is the total amount of memory being used; compiler temporary arrays may be very large, requiring a large main memory. The second is that without proper management of compiler temporary arrays, the machine performance may suffer.

This chapter discusses the topic of managing compiler temporary arrays. Here we discuss strategies such as modifying or restricting certain transformations to help with the storage management problem, and we discuss problems and insights with compiling for different architectures.

---

```
do I = 1, N
    do J = 1, M
        do K = 1, P
            T = A(I,J,K) * B(I,J,K)
            C(I,J,K) = T*2
            D(I,J) = D(I,J) + T
        enddo
    enddo
enddo
```

**Figure 9.1.** Loop where scalar expansion creates a compiler temporary array for the scalar T.

---

## 9.1 Sources of Compiler Temporary Arrays

Several of the transformations performed for array-oriented machines create compiler temporary arrays. *Scalar expansion* [Wolf78] is one such transformation. Scalar expansion changes a scalar variable that is assigned in a loop into a temporary array variable. For example, the loop in Figure 9.1 will be transformed by full scalar expansion into:

```
do I = 1, N
    do J = 1, M
        do K = 1, P
            TT(I,J,K) = A(I,J,K) * B(I,J,K)
            C(I,J,K) = TT(I,J,K)*2
            D(I,J) = D(I,J) + TT(I,J,K)
        enddo
    enddo
enddo
```

The scalar T is "expanded" into the three-dimensional array TT. The advantage of scalar expansion is that the parallelism in the loop is easier to discover, and the loops can be distributed and vectorized.

Another transformation that creates compiler generated arrays is the simple parsing of array-language expressions. In order to compute the expression below:

```
A(1:N,1:M) = B(1:N,1:M) + C(1:N,1:M) + D(1:N,1:M)
```

a compiler generated array can be used to hold the value of the subexpression:

```
T(1:N,1:M) = B(1:N,1:M) + C(1:N,1:M)
A(1:N,1:M) = T(1:N,1:M) + D(1:N,1:M)
```

An alternate way to compute this expression is to transform the array syntax into serial loops and use a scalar temporary:

```
do I = 1, N
    do J = 1, M
        T = B(I,J) + C(I,J)
        A(I,J) = T + D(I,J)
    enddo
enddo
```

Some array expressions, such as the one below, require a compiler generated array for proper execution; this was shown in Chapter 5:

```
A(2:N-1,2:M-1) = (A(1:N-2,2:M-1) + A(3:N,2:M-1)
                + A(2:N-1,1:M-2) + A(2:N-1,3:M)) / 4
```

## 9.2 Reducing the Size of Compiler Generated Arrays

Wherever compiler temporary arrays are generated, they can be very large - several dimensions with each dimension being as long as the trip count of a **do** loop. One way to reduce the impact of large compiler generated arrays is to use dynamic memory allocation. The temporary array could be allocated as needed and deallocated after use. The disadvantage of this approach is the overhead of the allocation and deallocation process.

Another method is to use a compiler temporary pool. The temporary space pool is a large block of memory that is requested once and reused many times in different ways throughout a program. If this is done carefully, a single temporary space pool could be used for a whole program composed of many subroutines, instead of a separate temporary pool for each subroutine. This can be more efficient that dynamically requesting memory from the operating system each time a temporary array is needed, although essentially the two methods are equivalent.

Neither of these two methods reduces the size of individual compiler generated arrays. This can be done by modifying the transformations that generate the arrays. Scalar expansion can be modified to only expand scalars for the innermost loop, creating a one dimensional array. Vector expressions can be transformed to their serial equivalent (as shown in Chapter 5) and scalar or single dimensional temporary variables can be created; this can not always be done, but in most cases it is possible. This way the total amount of compiler generated array space can be kept small while still allowing vector code to be generated.

For example, the loop below shows how the loop in Figure 9.1 would look if scalar expansion were modified to only expand scalars for the innermost loop. This compiler generated array needs only P storage locations, instead of N*M*P locations for a three dimensional temporary array:

```
do I = 1, N
    do J = 1, M
        do K = 1, P
            TT(K) = A(I,J,K) * B(I,J,K)
            C(I,J,K) = TT(K)*2
            D(I,J) = D(I,J) + TT(K)
        enddo
    enddo
enddo
```

However, this will not allow the best vector code to be generated. By restricting scalar expansion as above, loop interchanging will also be affected. In fact, if scalars are expanded into single dimensional arrays, and loops are then interchanged, the inner loop will usually not be vectorizable.

## 9.3 Array Contraction

There is a way to reduce the size of compiler generated arrays without affecting loop interchanging. We want to allow scalar expansion to fully expand scalars in order to be able to
compute better data dependence graphs and in order to allow loop interchanging to choose the
best loop ordering without unnecessary constraints. After the loops are interchanged and distributed, however, there is no reason to keep unnecessarily large compiler temporary arrays
around. Thus, the compiler can perform *Array Contraction*. This is effectively the inverse of
scalar expansion; where scalar expansion adds subscripts to scalars, array contraction removes
subscripts from arrays. In the limit, array contraction can change a compiler generated array
back into a scalar temporary.

There are only two rules for array contraction:
1) Subscripts that are used to carry values from one loop to another must not be removed.
2) Subscripts that are used in a vector or parallel way must not be removed.

All other subscripts may be removed. These rules take advantage of the way compiler
temporary arrays are generated, and the fact that they are indexed in a simple manner (one loop
corresponds to one subscript).

*Example.* The loop below is Figure 9.1 after full scalar expansion, loop interchanging and
vectorization of the **do** I loop:

```
do J = 1, M
   do K = 1, P
      TT(1:N,J,K) = A(1:N,J,K) * B(1:N,J,K)
      C(1:N,J,K) = TT(1:N,J,K)*2
      D(1:N,J) = D(1:N,J) + TT(1:N,J,K)
   enddo
enddo
```

Since the first subscript of the compiler generated array T is used in a vector manner, it cannot
be deleted; however the second and third subscripts can be deleted, reducing the size of T to
only N elements:

```
do J = 1, M
   do K = 1, P
      TT(1:N) = A(1:N,J,K) * B(1:N,J,K)
      C(1:N,J,K) = TT(1:N)*2
      D(1:N,J) = D(1:N,J) + TT(1:N)
   enddo
enddo
```

**Contraction of User Variables.** Array contraction can also be performed on programmer
array variables in certain cases. If a programmer array is subscripted simply, like a compiler
generated array, and if it is local to the subroutine being compiled (not a parameter, not an

146

external name, and not in a Fortran COMMON block) then it may be a candidate for array con-traction. While array contraction will have little effect (applied to programmer arrays) when compiling serial languages, it can be useful when compiling array syntax. Programmers using array languages may use array temporary variables and these may be (like compiler generated arrays) unnecessarily large. This is especially true when compiling array languages for serial machines.

*Example.* If the array assignment below:

```
A(2:N,2:M)  =  B(2:N,2:M)  *  2
C(2:N,2:M)  =  A(2:N,2:M)  +  D(2:N,2:M)
```

were compiled for a machine with one-dimensional vector instructions, then one dimension of the array syntax would be translated into serial loops (and presumably fused):

```
do I = 2, M
    A(2:N,I)  =  B(2:N,I)  *  2
    C(2:N,I)  =  A(2:N,I)  +  D(2:N,I)
enddo
```

Assuming that the array A was not used anywhere else in the program (it is a user temporary), then it could be contracted, resulting in:

```
do I = 2, M
    A(2:N)    =  B(2:N,I)  *  2
    C(2:N,I)  =  A(2:N)    +  D(2:N,I)
enddo
```

Notice that array contraction not only saves memory space but eliminates the code necessary to do the indexing for those subscripts which are deleted, a small savings in execution time.

## 9.4 Restricting Loop Distribution to Improve Array Contraction

The amount of array contraction possible is limited by the amount of loop distribution (or vec-torization) done. If a loop is distributed so that the assignment and use of a compiler generated array are in distinct loops, then the subscript of the array that corresponds to that loop cannot be deleted. If two loops are distributed thus, then the array will require two dimensions, one for each loop.

To counteract this effect, loop distribution should be restricted so that it only distributes a small number of loops around statements which assign compiler generated arrays. "Small" here is machine dependent, but usually for machine with vector instructions there is no need to distribute or vectorize more than one loop around each statement. This must be taken into account when distributing loops both when required to do loop interchanging and when vector-izing inner loops.

## 9.5 Strip Mining

Some loops may have unknown (at compiler time) loop limits. Thus, the amount of space necessary for a compiler generated array may also be unknown at compile time. In these cases dynamic memory allocation support is required to do the type of compiler temporary usage discussed up to now. In an environment which does not have dynamic memory allocation, another compile time strategy can be employed.

The loops can be *strip mined,* either before or after compiler arrays are generated; the strip-size can be chosen according to the machine architecture (64 in the case of Cray machines) or according to some cost/benefit function (large strips mean longer vector operations but more memory requirements).

Below we see the loop from Figure 9.1 with the inner loop strip mined to a size of 64. The compiler generated array now has a fixed size (64) and can be allocated statically at compile time:

```
do I = 1, N
    do J = 1, M
        do KS = 0, P-1, 64
            KL = MIN(64,P-KS)
            do K = 1, KL
                TT(K) = A(I,J,KS+K) * B(I,J,KS+K)
                C(I,J,KS+K) = TT(K)*2
                D(I,J) = D(I,J) + TT(K)
            enddo
        enddo
    enddo
enddo
```

## 9.6 Natural Solutions to Temporary Array Allocation

Some architectures have a natural solution to the compiler generated temporary array allocation problem. On a vector register machine, a temporary array can be implemented as a vector register without being allocated in memory at all. This results in a savings in memory space and in time, since the temporary array need not be stored from the vector register into memory.

On a multi-processor, a compiler generated array can be implemented as a local variable (or register) in each processor. Each processor then uses the temporary as a local scalar, and again a savings in time and space would result, since the temporary array would not need to be stored in the global memory.

## 9.7 Other Work in Compiler Temporary Array Management

Strip mining is designed to map long loops onto machines (like the Illiac-IV) that had a fixed amount of parallelism [Love77]. It is now used in all vectorizing compilers for vector register computers.

Dynamic memory allocation support is proposed in Fortran 8x; some current implementations already include support for it. If strip mining is used, then dynamic memory allocation is not needed. It is interesting to note that the Control Data Fortran 200 compiler has long offered dynamic memory allocation. This may be due to the fact that the Cyber 205 executes more efficiently with long vectors than with short vectors. Any transformation like strip mining which shortens the vector length severely affects the performance of the machine.

Some form of scalar expansion is used in most vectorizing compilers and translators. For compilers that vectorize only innermost loops, most of the problems associated with scalar expansion disappear.

An early treatment of full scalar expansion, creating a dimension for each loop that contains the assignment to the scalar, appears in [Lamp74]; he also mentions array contraction.

# 10  Vectorizing While Loops

All of the work so far in this text has been in the area of iterative **do** loops. An iterative **do** loop has a known (at execution) index set; the number of iterations of the loop can be computed when the loop is entered. This number is independent of the calculations inside the loop. Thus, if there is no branching in the loop and the loop has N iterations, then each statement in the loop will be executed exactly N times. This fact makes vectorization easy, since the vector length is fixed.

Not every loop has a fixed index set. We will classify any loop where the number of iterations is dependent on the calculations in the loop as a **while** loop. Three forms of this loop are immediately discernible. The first has the exit test at the top of the loop, as in a Pascal **while** loop:

```
while ( A > 1 ) do
    A = A / 2
    N = N + 1
endwhile
```

The second has the exit at the bottom of the loop, as in a Pascal REPEAT-UNTIL loop:

```
repeat
    XOLD = X
    X = F(X)
until ( ABS(XOLD-X) < TOL)
```

The third is an iterative **do** loop with an **if** test that conditionally branches out of the loop:

```
do I = 1, N
    A(I) = B(I) * D(I)
    if ( A(I) = 0 ) goto exitlabel
    C(I) = E(I) / A(I)
enddo
exitlabel:
```

Vectorizing **while** loops is difficult and often impossible. This chapter shows the problems and some proposed solutions in this area.

## 10.1 Changing While Loops into DO Loops

Some **while** loops can be dealt with very effectively. These are the cases where the **while** loop can be transformed directly into a **do** loop, as in:

```
I = 1
while ( I <= N ) do
    A(I) = B(I)
    I = I + 1
endwhile
```

which can be translated into:

```
do I = 1, N
    A(I) = B(I)
enddo
```

(assuming zero-trip **do** loops).  Notice that the **while** loop has an induction variable (I, in this case) and the loop exit tests that induction variable.

Some cases may have more than one exit condition, as in:

```
I = 1
while ( I <= N and B(I) > 0 ) do
    A(I) = B(I)
    I = I + 1
endwhile
```

Even translating the **while** loop into a **do** loop does not solve the **while** loop problem, since the new **do** loop still has a loop exit:

```
do I = 1, N
    if ( B(I) <= 0 ) goto exitlabel
    A(I) = B(I)
enddo
exitlabel:
```

Note that there may also have to be some cleaning up with respect to the last value assigned to the induction variable(s) of the loop.

## 10.2 Loop Exit IFs

Any **do** loop with an **if** that conditionally branches out of the loop falls into the category of a loop with an exit **if**.  There are many problems with simply vectorizing a **do** loop with an exit **if**.  The next section gives a special case of an exit **if** that can be handled more efficiently than general loop exit **if**s.

The first problem with vectorizing a **do** loop with an exit **if** (assuming there is no data dependence cycle that prevents vectorization) is that the resulting vectorized code may take longer to execute that the original serial code. If the simple loop below:

```
do I = 1, N
   A(I) = B(I)*C(I) + 4/D(I)
   if( A(I) = S(I) ) goto label
enddo
```

were simplistically vectorized, the following code might result:

```
A(1:N) = B(1:N)*C(1:N) + 4/D(1:N)
bit(1:N) = A(1:N) = S(1:N)
I = First1(bit(1:N))
if( I > 0 ) goto label
```

If N is large, but the loop exit condition is satisfied for some small I, say I = 2, then the serial version will execute only 2 iterations of the loop, while the vectorized version will execute all iterations of each statement before finding that the last N−2 iterations were unnecessary

The second problem with vectorizing a **do** loop with an exit **if** is that the vectorized version may store invalid results and thus will behave differently than the serial program. Using the above loop as an example again, if the exit condition were met for I = 2, then in the serial version the array A is left unchanged for elements A(3) to A(N). The vectorized version overwrites all elements of A, however. If these values are used later in the execution of the program, then the behavior of the program may change. One way to solve this problem is to assign all results computed in the loop to compiler temporary arrays. After the loop exit point is found, the proper results can be copied to the program variables:

```
ATEMP(1:N) = B(1:N)*C(1:N) + 4/D(1:N)
bit(1:N) = ATEMP(1:N) = S(1:N)
I = First1(bit(1:N))
if( I > 0 ) goto label
A(1:I) = ATEMP(1:I)
```

The third problem with vectorizing **do** loops with exit **if**s is spurious arithmetic faults. Even in the example code above where invalid stores were prevented, the vectorized version does some computation that the serial version does not. If the exit condition were met for I = 2, then the vectorized version would still compute B(I)*C(I)+4/D(I) for I = 3, ..., N. This computation could produce any of several arithmetic faults, such as overflow, underflow or divide by zero, which would not occur in the serial version. Ignoring all such faults in the vectorized version would also ignore the faults produced for the cases when the serial version would also fault, and so is generally unsatisfactory. If extra hardware support is available to save the faults with the temporary result array and to raise the fault when the results are copied to the actual arrays, this problem may be alleviated. As in any vectorized loop, the faults may be raised in a different order than they would be for the serial loops. There is also always the potential of adding lots of temporary array storage and a significant amount of time spent just copying values.

Loop distribution can be used to split out those parts of the loop upon which the exit test is dependent. In the loop below:

```
        do I = 1, N
S₁:         A(I) = B(I)*C(I) + 4/D(I)
S₂:         G(I) = H(I)*A(I)
S₃:         if( A(I) = S(I) ) goto label
        enddo
```

only the values computed in $S_1$ are needed in the loop exit test. Loop distribution can be used to split $S_2$ into a separate loop:

```
        LASTI = 0
        LASTI2 = 0
        do I = 1, N
            LASTI = I
S₁:         A(I) = B(I)*C(I) + 4/D(I)
S₃:         if( A(I) = S(I) ) goto exitlabel
            LASTI2 = I
        enddo
exitlabel:
        do J = 1, LASTI
S₂:         G(J) = H(J)*A(J)
        enddo
        if( LASTI ≠ LASTI2 ) goto label
```

Now, the second loop can be vectorized with none of the problems mentioned above. The first loop can either be left serial, or some more dangerous technique can be used.

## 10.3 Error Exit IFs

A certain class of loop exit **if**s deserves special mention. In many standard algorithms (such as Gaussian elimination) a test is made in a loop for some unexpected and/or illegal condition (such as non-singular matrix). Should this case arise, the program generally stops, since the input was invalid. In these cases it may be possible to allow the vectorized program to overwrite the program variables, instead of using compiler temporary arrays, since the only cases when the loop exit will be taken is when the input is in error anyway. Basically this type of loop exit is one of low probability that signals user error, so the transformed program does not need to behave exactly as the original program.

Unfortunately, there is no way for a compiler to spot which loop exit **if**s are error exits and which are not. Some heuristics may be applied (based on the types of error exit **if** found in common subroutine packages, such as EISPACK), but no safe decision can be made without some additional input from the programmer.

## 10.4 General While Loops

Attempting to vectorize general **while** loops (or Repeat-Until loops) is even more frustrating than vectorizing loops with exit **if**s. In a general **while** loop, there is no indication of the number of iterations that will be executed or are expected by the programmer to be executed. The vector length cannot be decided even at execution time before the loop is already executed.

An artificial vector length can be introduced by strip mining the **while** loop. The **while** loop below:

```
while ( X > EPS ) do
    X = F(X)
endwhile
```

can be strip mined:

```
while ( X > EPS ) do
    XTEMP(0) = X
    do I = 1, 64
        XTEMP(I) = F(XTEMP(I-1))
    enddo
    bit(1:64) = XTEMP(1:64) > EPS
    J = First1( bit(1:64) )
    X = XTEMP(J)
endwhile
```

Some number of iterations of the statements in the **while** loop (64 iterations in this example) are executed before any testing is done. The hope is that this computation is vectorizable; if it is not vectorizable, then the original **while** loop should be executed serially. After 64 iterations of the statements in the **while** loop, a test are made to see if any of the iterations just completed satisfy the exit condition. If so, those results are saved and the loop is exited.

As can be seen, vectorizing **while** loops is a difficult process. All the problems that arose in dealing with exit **if**s arise here also: possibly increasing execution time, storing invalid results and spurious arithmetic faults. This process is further complicated by the almost universal appearance of a recurrence relation in **while** loops in scientific programs. If a **while** loop contains a non-vectorizable recurrence relation, then no amount of fiddling with the **while** loop will remove the recurrence.

As with exit **if**s, loop fission can be used to split out parts of the **while** loop which are not used in the exit condition. The **while** loop can thereby be split into the **while** part, which computes a vector length, and a **do** part, which executes for the number of iterations. The **do** part can be vectorized with conventional techniques.

One class of **while** loops can be translated more efficiently than general **while** loops. These are **while** loops which test some convergent condition. By "convergent", we mean that once the exit condition is satisfied, further iterations of the loop will always satisfy the condition; in fact, more iterations may produce a better (more desirable to the programmer) answer. A simpler strip mining scheme can be employed which would produce more efficient code. The **while** loop above could be strip mined more efficiently if the **while** condition were "convergent":

```
while ( X > EPS ) do
    XTEMP(0) = X
    do I = 1, 64
        XTEMP(I) = F(XTEMP(I-1))
    enddo
    X = XTEMP(64)
endwhile
```

Unfortunately, no compiler can tell from the source code alone (of any language today) whether a particular **while** condition is a convergence test.

## 10.5 Interchanging DO Loops and While Loops

If a **while** loop is enclosed in a **do** loop, and if the **while** loop can be interchanged with the **do** loop, then the **do** loop may be vectorized and the **while** loop can be executed serially. This procedure would seem to solve most of the problems with **while** loops in the cases where it applies; in fact, it does solve most of them, but not all.

The **while** loop below is enclosed in a **do** loop:

```
do I = 1, N
    while ( X(I) > 1 ) do
        X(I) = F(X(I))
    endwhile
enddo
```

With the loops properly interchanged, this becomes:

```
while ( ANY(X(1:N) > 1) ) do
    do I = 1, N
        if (X(I) > 1) X(I) = F(X(I))
    enddo
endwhile
```

To ensure that each iteration of the **do** loop is executed until it satisfies the **while** condition, the new **while** condition must be satisfied for all iterations of the loop simultaneously. To be sure that each iteration of the **do** loop is not executed after the **while** condition is satisfied for the iteration, an **if** test must be added.

The problem is that in the original loop, the **while** condition may be satisfied in just a few iterations for most I and may take a long time for only a few I. In the interchanged loop, the **do** loop is executed for its entire index set for each iteration of the **while** loop until all the

**while** conditions are satisfied. Thus, the total amount of execution may again increase. There is no problem of spurious errors or storing invalid values, however.

If the **while** condition is "convergent", then the **if** clause need not be added. In this case, the **do** loop will be executed for all I until all iterations satisfy the convergence condition. Some of the answers may be "better" than would be obtained by the original program, but the execution time may still increase in certain cases.

## 10.6 Concurrentizing While Loops

Some work has been done on executing **while** loops concurrently across multiple processors. The technique boils down to finding a critical section which decides whether to start the next iteration. This critical section is made as small as possible and is moved to the top of the loop. The hope is that there is enough code in the loop outside of the critical section to get good speedup. It is a similar idea to vectorizing a **while** loop by distributing out the statements that do not affect the **while** condition. At least one commercial compiler automatically concurrentizes **while** loops.

## 10.7 Conclusions

Vectorizing **while** loops is a tricky business. No current vectorizer even attempts this, except to change **while** loops into **do** loops. There are cases where leaving the **while** loop as a serial loop seems to be the best choice. New machine architecture developments may affect the way these loops are handled in the future. In any case, dealing with **while** loops will not be as automatic a process as vectorizing **do** loops; there is much special knowledge that is required from the programmer for the compiler to do the best job.

# 11   Structure of a Supercompiler

Many of the same optimizations can be applied to different supercomputers. Optimization phases of compilers for different supercomputers can all have the same general structure. Here I propose a general structure around which to design an optimizing supercompiler. I do this with the benefit of experience gained while working on the Parafrase Analyzer, and with a commercial derivative, KAP from Kuck and Associates, Inc. I also have seen several successful and not so successful compiler designs for supercomputers in the past 5 years, and have some advice for new supercompiler designers.

Typically, a compiler consists of three phases:

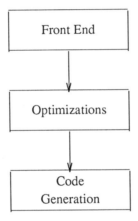

Much work has been done to make compilers with multiple front ends and multiple back ends, but which share (much of) the optimization phase. There is no reason to abandon this general design, though, of course, some of the optimizations are language or machine dependent. Typical optimizations are induction variable recognition, common subexpression elimination, and so on.

The optimizations described here should be thought of as "high-level" optimizations; that is, they transform the high level specification of the program. As such, they should be performed before the scalar optimizations:

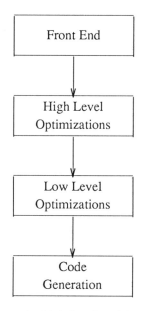

There may be some overlap between the high level and low level optimizations; for instance, induction variable recognition is important both for vectorization and for scalar code generation.

In general, the scope of the optimization is quite different. For high level optimizations, the compiler needs to know things like loops, arrays and subscripts. For low level optimizations, the array subscripting code can be lowered and loops may turn into **ifs** and **goto**s. A common mistake seen when a vectorizer is inserted into a compiler design is that the front end already lowers the code for array accesses and loops, making the job for the vectorizer just that much harder, and sometimes entirely impractical. More successful designs have a high level program representation for the high level optimizations, then code lowering is performed before scalar optimizations.

**Future Compilers.** It is unclear how compilers will be used ten years hence. It will certainly be as important as ever to be able to perform as much optimization as possible automatically. There is also a great deal of research being done on programming environments, which would change the way programs are written, maintained and executed. Environments can allow compilers to interact with the user, and might even allow run-time information to feed back into the optimization phase for subsequent runs.

**User Training.** It may be hard to retrain users away from the "black box" compiler mode. However, compiler writers already have some experience training users. Vectorizing compilers reward "good behavior" by marking those loops as "vectorized", and punish "bad behavior" by pointing out those nasty phrases that can't be vectorized. Users have become accustomed to vectorizers, and have become well trained, writing programs that will be acceptable to the particular vectorizer they are using. As compilers get more sophisticated, it becomes more important to think of training users both to understand what the compiler did or can do, and to understand how to get the compiler to generate efficient code.

**Debugging.** Some of the high level optimizations make major modifications to the program. Normal debugging techniques, such as setting breakpoints and looking at variable values, may not be as simple when loops are distributed and interchanged, and variables get expanded, shrunk or renamed. This is still very much as area for research, partly because it is unclear what is the best way to interface to users, especially on multiprocessor computers.

**Further Optimizations.** At one point, I believed that after vectorization and concurrency detection, there were no more interesting compiler optimization problems. Obviously, I was young and naive. It seems the next optimization problem is dealing with the memory hierarchy. Scalar and vector registers, cache memories (both private and shared), local memories and large shared global memories all are levels of a memory hierarchy. Many machines today are designed with several of these levels; to get the best performance from the machine, it is important to keep data in the highest level in the hierarchy as long as possible. Some techniques, such as special iteration space tiling [Wolf87, IrTr88], seem to have potential to address this problem. Certainly, after memory hierarchies are no longer interesting, some other architectural feature of supercomputers will become a bottleneck, and will need some optimization, so compiler researchers can look forward to a long and interesting career.

# References

Ph.D. theses cited below are available from University Microfilms, Inc., Ann Arbor, Michigan, with the given UMI order number.

[AAGK86] Annaratone, M., E. Arnould, T. Gross, H. T. Kung, M. S. Lam, O. Menzilcioglu, K. Sarocky and J. A. Webb, "Warp Architecture and Implementation," *Proc. of the 13th Annual Int'l Symp. on Computer Architecture,* IEEE Computer Society Press, Los Angeles, CA, pp. 346-356, June, 1986.

[AbKL81] Abu-Sufah, W. A., D. J. Kuck and D. H. Lawrie, "On the Performance Enhancement of Paging Systems Through Program Analysis and Transformations," *IEEE Trans. on Computers,* Vol. C-30, No. 5, pp. 341-356, May 1981.

[AbuS78] Abu-Sufah, W. A., *Improving the Performance of Virtual Memory Computers,* Ph.D. Thesis, Univ. of Ill. at Urbana-Champaign, Dept. of Comp. Sci. Rpt. No. 78-945, (UMI 79-15307), Nov. 1978.

[AhSU86] Aho, A. V., R. Sethi and J. D. Ullman, *Compilers: Principles, Techniques and Tools,* Addison-Wesley, Reading, MA, 1986.

[AlCK87] Allen, R., D. Callahan and K. Kennedy, "Automatic Decomposition of Scientific Programs for Parallel Execution," *Proc. of the 14th Annual ACM Symp. on Principles of Programming Languages,* pp. 63-76, Jan. 1987.

[AlCo72] Allen, F. E. and J. Cocke, "A Catalogue of Optimizing Transformations," *Design and Optimization of Compilers,* R. Rustin (ed.), Prentice-Hall, Englewood Cliffs, NJ, pp. 1-30, 1972.

[AlKe84] Allen, J. R. and K. Kennedy, "Automatic Loop Interchange," *Proc. of the ACM SIGPLAN '84 Symposium on Compiler Construction,* Montreal, Canada, June 17-22, 1984; *SIGPLAN Notices,* Vol. 19, No. 6, pp. 233-246, June, 1984.

[AlKe85] Allen, J. R. and K. Kennedy, "A Parallel Programming Environment," *IEEE Software,* Vol. 2, No. 4, pp. 21-29, July, 1985.

[AlKe87] Allen, J. R. and K. Kennedy, "Automatic Translation of Fortran Programs to Vector Form," *ACM Transactions on Programming Languages and Systems,* Vol. 9, No. 4, pp. 491-542, Oct. 1987.

[Alle83]     Allen, J. R., *Dependence Analysis for Subscripted Variables and Its Application to Program Transformations,* Ph.D. Thesis, Rice Univ. (UMI 83-14916), Houston, TX, April, 1983.

[Alli86]     *FX/Fortran Language Manual, Vol. 1: Guidelines* Alliant Computer Corporation, Littleton, MA, Nov. 1986.

[ANSI87]    *X3J3 Draft Fortran Standard,* American National Standard Institute, 1987.

[BaCK80]   Banerjee, U., D. Gajski and D. J. Kuck, "Array Machine Control Units for Loops Containing IFs," *Proc. of the 1980 Int'l Conf. on Parallel Processing,* Harbor Springs, MI, pp. 28-36, Aug. 1980.

[Bane76]    Banerjee, U., "Data Dependence in Ordinary Programs," M.S. Thesis, Univ. of Ill. at Urbana-Champaign, Dept. of comp. Sci. Rpt. No. 76-837, Nov. 1976.

[Bane79]    Banerjee, U., *Speedup of Ordinary Programs,* Ph.D. Thesis, Univ. of Ill. at Urbana-Champaign, Dept. of Comp. Sci. Rpt. No. 79-989, (UMI 80-08967), Oct. 1979.

[BCKT79]   Banerjee, U., S. C. Chen, D. J. Kuck and R. A. Towle, "Time and Parallel Processor Bounds for Fortran-Like Loops," *IEEE Trans. on Computers,* Vol. C-28, No. 9, pp. 660-670, Sept. 1979.

[BuCy86]    Burke, M. and R. Cytron, "Interprocedural Dependence Analysis and Parallelization," *Proc. of the SIGPLAN '86 Symposium on Compiler Construction,* Palo Alto, CA, pp. 162-175, June 1986.

[ChKu75]   Chen, S. C. and K. J. Kuck, "Time and Parallel Processor Bounds for Linear Recurrence Systems," *IEEE Trans. on Computers,* pp. 701-717, July 1975.

[CoDa81]   *CDC Cyber 200 Model 205 compute System, Hardware Reference Manual,* Control Data Corporation, Pub. No. 60256020, rev. A, March 1981.

[CoDa84]   *Cyber 200 Fortran Language 1.5., Reference Manual,* Control Data Corporation, Pub. No. 60480200, rev. D, Mar. 1984.

[Cray86]    *Cray-X-MP and Cray-1 Computer Systems Fortran (CFT) Reference Manual,* Cray Research, Inc., Pub. No. SR-0009, rev. L, Feb. 1986.

[Cytr84]   Cytron, R. G., *Compile Time Scheduling and Optimization for Asynchronous Machines,* Ph.D. Thesis, Univ. of Ill. at Urbana-Champaign, Dept. of Comp. Sci. Rpt. No. 84-1177, (UMI 85-02121), Oct. 1984.

[Cytr86]   Cytron, R. G., "Doacross: Beyond Vectorization for Multiprocessors," *Proc. of the 1986 Int'l Conf. on Parallel Processing,* Hwang, Jacobs, Swartzlander (eds.), IEEE Computer Society Press, Los Angeles, CA, pp 836-844, Aug. 1986.

[Cytr87]   Cytron, R., "Limited Processing Scheduling of Doacross Loops," *Proc. of the 1987 Int'l Conf. on Parallel Processing,* Sahni (ed.), Penn State Univ. Press, University Park, PA, pp. 226-234, Aug. 1987.

[Davi81]   Davies, J. R. B., "Parallel Loop Constructs for Multiprocessors," M.S. Thesis, Univ. of Ill. at Urbana-Champaign, Dept. of Comp. Sci. Rpt. No. 81-1070, May 1981.

[Elli85]   Ellis, J. R., *Bulldog: A Compiler for VLIW Architectures,* Ph.D. Thesis, Yale University, The MIT Press, Cambridge, MA, 1985.

[FeOW87]  Ferrante, J., K. J. Ottenstein and J. D. Warren, "The Program Dependence Graph and Its Use in Optimization," *ACM Transactions on Programming Languages and Systems,* Vol. 9, No. 3, pp. 319-349, July 1987.

[Grif54]   Griffin, H., *Elementary Theory of Numbers,* McGraw-Hill, New York, NY, 1954.

[HeLi82]   Heuft, R. W. and W. D. Little, "Improved Time and Parallel Processor Bounds for Fortran-Like Loops," *IEEE Transactions on Computers,* Vol. C-31, No. 1, pp. 78-81, Jan. 1982.

[IrTr88]   Irigoin F. and R. Triolet, "Supernode Partitioning," *Proc. of the 15th Annual ACM Symp. on Principles of Programming Languages,* San Diego, CA, pp. 319-329, Jan. 1988.

[KCPS8]   Kuck, D. J., A. H. Sameh, R. Cytron, A. V. Veidenbaum, C. D. Polychronopoulos, G. Lee, T. McDaniel, B. R. Leasure, C. Beckman, J. R. B. Davies and C. P. Kruskal, "The Effects of Program Restructuring, Algorithm Change and Architecture Choice on Program Performance," *Proc. of the 1984 Int'l Conf. on Parallel Processing,* Keller (ed.), IEEE Computer Society Press, Washington, DC, pp. 129-138, Aug. 1984.

[Kenn80]   Kennedy, K., "Automatic Translation of Fortran Programs to Vector Form," Rice
Technical Report 476-029-4, Rice University, Houston, Oct. 1980.

[Kirc74]   Kirch, A. M., *Elementary Number Theory,* Intext, New York, NY, 1974.

[KKLW80] Kuck, D. J., R. H. Kuhn, B. Leasure and M. Wolfe, "The Structure of an Advanced
Vectorizer for Pipelined Processors," *Proc. of COMPSAC 80, The 4th Interna-
tional Computer Software and Applications Conf.,* Chicago, IL, pp. 709-715, Oct.
1980.

[KKPL81]  Kuck, D. J., R. H. Kuhn, D. A. Padua, B. Leasure and M. Wolfe, "Dependence
Graphs and Compiler Optimizations," *Proc. of the 8th ACM Symp. on of Programming Languages (POPL),* Williamsburg, VA, pp. 207-218, Jan. 1981.

[KPSW81]  Kuck, D. J., D. A. Padua, A. H. Sameh and M. Wolfe, "Languages and High-
Performance Computations," *Proc. of the IFIP IC2 Working Conf. on the Relation-
ship between Numerical Computation and Programming Languages,* pp. 205-219,
Aug. 1981.

[Kuhn80]   Kuhn, R. H., *Optimization and Interconnection Complexity for: Parallel Processors, Single-Stage Networks, and Decision Trees,* Ph.D. Thesis, Univ. of Ill. at
Urbana-Champaign, Dept. of Comp. Sci. Rpt. No. 80-1009, (UMI 80-26541), Feb.
1980.

[Lamp74]   Lamport, L., "The Parallel Execution of DO Loops," *Comm. of the ACM,* pp. 83-
93, Feb. 1974.

[Leas76]   Leasure, B. R., "Compiling Serial Languages for Parallel Machines," M.S. Thesis,
Univ. of Ill. at Urbana-Champaign, Dept. of Comp. Sci. Rpt. No. 76-805, Nov.
1976.

[Love77]   Loveman, D. B., "Program Improvement by Source-to-Source Transformation," *J.
of the ACM,* Vol. 20, No. 1, pp. 121-145, Jan. 1977.

[LuBa80]   Lundstrom, S. F. and G. H. Barnes, "A Controllable MIMD Architecture," *Proc.
1980 Int' l Conf. of Parallel Processing,* IEEE Computer Soc., pp. 19-27, 1980.

[MiPa86]   Midkiff, S. P. and D. A. Padua, "Compiler Generated Synchronization for DO
Loops," *Proc. of the 1986 Int'l Conf. on Parallel Processing,* IEEE Computer
Society Press, Washington, DC, pp. 554-551, Aug. 1986.

[MiPa87]  Midkiff, S. P. and D. A. Padua, "Compiler Algorithms for Synchronization," *IEEE Trans. on Computers,* Vol. C-36, No. 12, pp. 1485-1495, Dec. 1987.

[Mura71]  Muraoka, Y., *Parallelism Exposure and Exploitation in Programs,* Ph.D. Thesis, Univ. of Ill. at Urbana-Champaign, Dept. of Comp. Sci. Rpt. No. 71-424, (UMI 71-21189), Feb. 1971.

[Padu79]  Padua, D. *Multiprocessors: Discussions of some Theoretical and Practical Problems,* Ph.D. Thesis, Univ. of Ill. at Urbana-Champaign, Dept. of Comp. Sci. Rpt. No. 79-990, Nov. 1979.

[PaKL80]  Padua, D. A., D. J. Kuck and D. H. Lawrie, "High-Speed Multiprocessors and Compilation Techniques," *IEEE Trans. on Computers,* Vol C-29, No. 9, pp. 763-776, Sep. 1980.

[PoKu87]  Polychronopoulos, C. D. and D. J. Kuck, "Guided Self-Scheduling: A Practical Scheduling Scheme for Parallel Supercomputers," *IEEE Trans. on Computers,* Vol. C-36, No. 12, pp. 1425-1439, Dec. 1987.

[Poly87]  Polychronopoulos, C. D., "Loop Coalescing: A Compiler Transformation for Parallel Machines," *Proc. of the 1987 Int'l Conf. on Parallel Processing,* Sahni (ed.), Penn State Univ. Press, University Park, PA, pp. 235-242, Aug. 1987.

[SaBr77]  Sameh, A. H. and R. P. Brent, "Solving Triangular Systems on a Parallel Computer," *SIAM J. Numer. Anal.,* Vol. 14, No. 6, pp. 1101-1113, Dec. 1977.

[Seit85]  Seitz, C. L., "The Cosmic Cube," *Comm. of the ACM,* Vol 28, No. 1, pp. 22-33, Jan. 1985.

[Sequ87]  *Guide to Parallel Programming,* Sequent Computer Systems, Beaverton, OR, 1987.

[Tarj72]  Tarjan, R., "Depth-First Search and Linear Graph Algorithms," *SIAM J. Comput.,* Vol. 1, No. 2, pp. 146-160, June. 1972.

[Towl76]  Towle, R. A., *Control and Data Dependence for Program Transformations,* Ph.D. Thesis, Univ. of Ill. at Urbana-Champaign, Dept. of Comp. Sci. Rpt. No. 76-788, (UMI 76-24191), Mar. 1976.

[Wall88]   Wallace, D., "Dependence of Multi-Dimensional Array References" to appear *Proc. of the 1988 ACM Int'l Conf. on Supercomputing,* Saint-Malo, France, July 1988.

[Wolf78]   Wolfe, M. J., "Techniques for Improving the Inherent Parallelism in Programs," M.S. Thesis, Univ. of Ill. at Urbana-Champaign, Dept. of Comp. Sci. Rpt. No. 78-929, July 1978.

[Wolf82]   Wolfe, M. J., *Optimizing Supercompilers for Supercomputers,* Ph.D. Thesis, Univ. of Ill. at Urbana-Champaign, Dept. of Comp. Sci. Rpt. No. 82-1105, (UMI 82-03027), Oct. 1982.

[Wolf87]   Wolfe, M. J., "Iteration Space Tiling for Memory Hierarchies," to appear in *Proc. of the 3rd SIAM Conf. on Parallel Processing,* Los Angeles, CA, Dec. 1987.